Also by Sherry Suib Cohen

Southern Beauty
(with Kylene Barker Brandon)

Cristina Ferrare Style
(with Cristina Ferrare DeLorean)

About Face
(with Jeffrey Bruce)

Diabetes
(with Lee Ducat)

Making It Big
(with Jean DuCoffe)

Tough Gazoobies on That!

SHERRY SUIB COHEN

QUIZZICAL PURSUITS

24 Quizzes to Test Yourself and Discover the Real You

A FIRESIDE BOOK
Published by Simon & Schuster, Inc.
New York

Most of the articles contained in this book have been previously published in *Playgirl* magazine.

Copyright © 1981, 1982, 1983, 1984 by Sherry Suib Cohen
All rights reserved
including the right of reproduction
in whole or in part in any form
A Fireside Book
Published by Simon & Schuster, Inc.
Simon & Schuster Building
Rockefeller Center
1230 Avenue of the Americas
New York, New York 10020
FIRESIDE and colophon are registered trademarks of
Simon & Schuster, Inc.
Designed by Pat Dunbar
Manufactured in the United States of America
Printed and bound by Fairfield Graphics

1 3 5 7 9 10 8 6 4 2

Library of Congress Cataloging in Publication Data
Cohen, Sherry Suib.
Quizzical Pursuits.

"A Fireside book."
1. Personality tests. 2. Love—Testing.
3. Work—Psychological aspects—Testing. I. Title.
BF698.5.C64   1984   155.2′8   84-13865
ISBN: 0-671-53070-4

Acknowledgments

With thanks to Dianne Grosskopf, Pat McGilligan, and my other editors at *Playgirl* magazine; the encouragement and freedom they gave me prompted the monthly column where many of these quizzes first appeared.

And thanks to my psychiatrist, psychologist, and lay analyst pals on whose ideas, advice, and assorted lunacies these quizzes drew.

And thanks to my parents, children, and husband—and to my agent, irrepressible Connie Clausen—whose lives always provide such great material.

And especially thanks to my Simon & Schuster editors, Deborah Chiel, who first saw that Quizzical Pursuits would be more easily done in a book of quizzes than on a psychiatrist's couch; and Susan Victor, who is nothing less than terrific!

Contents

Introduction 9

YOU

1. Do You Do It with Style? 13
2. Do You Show Grace Under Pressure? 19
3. Are You a Spontaneous Person? 24
4. Do You Have Street Smarts? 31
5. Are You Your Own Worst Enemy? 38
6. Is Your Health in Jeopardy? 44
7. Are You a Survivor? 50
8. How Far Have You Come in Ten Years? 56

YOU AND HOW YOU PLAY WITH OTHERS

9. How Well Do You Deal with Criticism? 63
10. Can You Hear What Others Are *Not* Saying? 69
11. Are You a Good Listener? 75
12. What's Your Love Style? 81
13. How Well Do You Communicate
    Your Sexual Desires? 87

8

14. How Much Do You Really Know About
    Your Man?   93
15. How Well Do You Fit into His Support System?   98
16. Have You Had It with Harry?   103

YOU AND HOW YOU WORK WITH OTHERS
17. Can You Ace an Interview?   113
18. What's Your Worth at Work?   120
19. Are You the Boss Type?   125
20. Should You Have an Office Romance?   131
21. Do You Have Job Burnout?   136
22. Are You a Good Credit Risk?   141
23. Will You Ever Be Really Rich?   147
24. Do You Have the Winner's Mystique?   152

Introduction

It seems, these days, that everyone is out to peg you, put a little label on you, and then sell you a book or self-help course on how to find the real you and, once having found it, how to fix it. Most of the so-called experts writing these books are more confounded by life than you are, but are nevertheless ready to give you a lecture and put you on an endless path to self-improvement.

The worst of it all, the inexcusable offense, is that these gurus who know what's best for you are so pontifical, so dull, so deadly *serious*. Would it kill them to relax and smile as they deliver their priceless advice?

The truth of the matter is that no one but you can really pinpoint *you*. Who knows better the real reasons for your choices in relationships, for your failures, your successes? No one. Deep inside, you not only know what each vulnerability is, you can spotlight your weaknesses instantly when you see them spread out on paper.

Which is why, since time immemorial, there has been no form of therapy as popular as the self-quiz. Quiz appeal transcends color, age, economic status, and intellectual level. Adam and Eve fooled around with quizzes—I'm *sure* of it! So did Alexander the Great. So does Seymour the Not-So-Great. Everyone loves a quiz because a good one will not only give you super entertainment, it will also very pointedly teach you something about yourself. We tend to spot our strengths and weaknesses more easily in a quiz than on an analyst's couch. We can then easily decide if we wish to do anything with the information.

However, here's the bad news: The quizzes one finds in most books, magazines, and newspapers tend to take themselves so seriously that they annul the good. They're written with the contention that human nature is not for laughs and when you want to talk about psyche, you'd better wipe that grin off your face.

Wrong. The best way to make a point to yourself is to make it lightly and that's why the quizzes in this book are irreverently funny, a little raunchy sometimes, as well as chockfull of insights and information you just might find useful.

Listen—your first-grade teacher knew what she was talking about when she gave you the D in "Works and Plays Well with Others." Getting along with others is all that counts, except, perhaps, that in order to work and play well with others, you have to be comfortable with yourself. That's why this collection is divided into three self-testing areas:

YOU

YOU AND HOW YOU PLAY WITH OTHERS

YOU AND HOW YOU WORK WITH OTHERS

In other words, you, your relationships, and your work arena. Is there anything else?

Take your time with these quizzes. Take them by yourself, with a buddy, with a lover. Use them as icebreakers to open up conversations about those hard-to-talk-about subjects. Have a laugh with them, but don't kid yourself: They're serious.

YOU

1

Do You Do It with Style?

You can be poor, handicapped, ugly—but if you do it with style, you're an interesting person! Style is *not* fashion or acceptability or the money you spend. Style is flare, color, excitement, good taste—*individuality*. Style is whatever you do that makes you unique. Style is a sense of class, a statement of *your* taste. If you "do it with style" you radiate security and intelligence, and above all you're not boring.

Do *you* do it with style?

1. SCENE: a crowded party. Your husband or lover has been slobbering over another woman all evening. You
   A. ignore it and stay cool.
   B. leave the party. Alone.
   C. try to get them to break up the scene by making it a three-way conversation, asking about her work, her plans.
   D. rake your nails lightly over his face.

2. A woman with style might wear sneakers with a sable coat because
   A. she really wants people to notice the coat.
   B. she really wants people to notice her tiny feet.

    C. she is impulsive, feels comfortable in sneakers and
       sable, and knows she can pull off any look at all.

    D. she stole the coat while she was out jogging.

3. A *sexual stylist* makes love as often as possible because
    A. she's trying to get it right.
    B. she's trying to find out what's new this season.
    C. she's trying to encourage a serious relationship.
    D. she's trying.

4. A person with real style never shouts and rarely even
   speaks above a very low voice because
    A. she wishes people to pay attention to her.
    B. she wishes people not to pay attention to her.
    C. she has private and confidential things to disclose.
    D. she has throat herpes.

5. You're a female student at Harvard. Your favorite thing
   to wear is
    A. a Harvard T-shirt.
    B. a Yale T-shirt.
    C. a shirt with an alligator on it.
    D. an alligator with a shirt on it.
    E. a clean (sometimes) shirt.
    F. a jock strap and high heels.

6. You and your lover are houseguests, and are enjoying a
   glorious night of making love. Your host's seven-year-old
   son wanders into your room in the midst of the festivities.
   You
    A. keep right on going because you're a free spirit and
       don't want him to think there's anything wrong with
       making love.
    B. laugh, decide to be playful, and pretend you're shoot-
       ing him with a gun.
    C. stop immediately, pull the covers over your head, and
       ask him if he likes school.
    D. tell him you'll meet him in the kitchen in a few min-
       utes to talk about it.

7. A rich aunt has left you with a whole lot of money to be
   spent "only on one year's entertainment." You spend it on

A. a series of intimate dinner parties given to enhance your professional and social standing.

B. a budget fund you put aside so you don't have to miss one well-reviewed movie or show this whole year.

C. whips, lashes, sticky things, handcuffs, nose plugs, antibiotic salves.

D. one gala, never-to-be-forgotten party.

8. You want something different in stationery. An artist friend offers to create an original line drawing for your notes. You choose

A. an etching of your expensive home and servants.

B. a large-eyed picture of your cocker spaniel.

C. a dramatic rendering of your initials.

D. a picture of something that *represents* you (a favorite hat, a book, or paintbrush).

E. a picture of Yasir Arafat.

9. You hate being poor mostly because

A. you can't pay your bills on time.

B. it embarrasses your friends.

C. you have to wear tacky clothes.

D. you have to think too much about money.

E. it sucks.

10. Something has come up and you can't make your date. Problem is, you're in a hurry and far from a telephone. Because you have style, you

A. don't show, don't send word (you can't help it), but the next day you send an armful of flowers and a nice note in apology.

B. notify your date even if you have to invent the telephone.

C. don't show, don't call, and never see the guy again because you feel so guilty.

11. A wealthy person with style

A. saves most of her money.

B. often apologizes for her wealth.

C. gives large sums of money to needy institutions.

D. spends much of her money on things that are fun.

12. A woman with style knows how to start a conversation. Which is the most stylish opener?
    A. "I see you're picking your nose. Would you like a Kleenex?"
    B. "Hi, my name is Marilyn. I just had my teeth cleaned and I hate to waste it."
    C. "What time is it?"
    D. "Do you have change for the telephone?"
    E. "That's an extraordinary watch (cologne, tie, etc.) you're wearing."

13. What statement about hair shows a woman of high style?
    A. "I'm blond because blonds have more fun."
    B. "I dyed the gray from my hair because I hate looking old."
    C. "I've colored my hair cherry red because that's what feels like *me*."
    D. "I hate hair. Hair makes you vulnerable. Hair makes you diseased."

ANSWERS AND ANALYSIS

1. A woman of real style would leave, *A*, because she has somewhere better to go—even if it's only home. She would kid no one by staying and make herself an object of pity—something no woman of style would stand for.

2. A woman of style is comfortable in looks that are unorthodox for most others. That's because her sense of style is in her head, *C*, not on her back or feet.

3. A woman of sexual style simply tries—everything, *D*. Why not? She has already gotten it right, couldn't care less what's accepted or popular this season, and doesn't have to *reach* for serious relationships.

4. A woman with style does like to be noticed, *A*. She knows that the best way to call attention to herself is with a whisper.

5. Style is not rejecting your own world or copying another's. It's being true to your own image. However, if you chose *F*, your style image is—*admit it*—confused.

6. Having flare and style doesn't mean being loutish or dumb. Any seven-year-old would think you were bananas if you didn't do something like *D*.

7. Style is the ability to create *panache, dazzle*. *A* is calculated but not stylish, *B* is plodding and unimaginative, and *C* is—well, each to her own entertainment; we just don't call it style.

8. *A* would really indicate a person who is the very opposite of stylish—gauche. Ditto for a *B* choice. *C* is not terrible; at least they're *your* initials. If you chose *E*, would he be wearing his beard stubble or not? It makes a difference!

9. Having to consume herself with thoughts of how to get and keep money would be a drag for a woman of true style. Such a woman would *never* wear tacky clothes (even if old and torn, they wouldn't be tacky) or even consider that her poverty might be embarrassing to anyone she found worthy to be a friend.

10. *Never could* a person of style stand anyone up without warning.

11. A stylish and wealthy woman would never apologize for her money. Nor would she give to faceless charities simply to create a philanthropic name for herself. She spends lustily, knowing that money is to have fun with, *D*, and gives to individuals whom she cares about.

12. *C* and *D* are openers for losers, not people of style. *B* is somewhat schmaltzy but it might work. *A* is not too sophisticated an opener. *E* opens up all kinds of possibilities for responses.

13. *A* and *B* are not truly stylish because they follow society's dictates. *D* is not only not stylish, she needs treatment very quickly. *C* is a woman making a statement about *herself*; that's true style.

SCORING

Figure out your score by using the number credits listed here. The preceding analysis gives the reasoning behind the scoring.

1. (A) 2	2. (A) 1	3. (A) 0	4. (A) 3	5. (A) 2	6. (A) 0	7. (A) 1
(B) 3	(B) 0	(B) 0	(B) 0	(B) 0	(B) 0	(B) 0
(C) 0	(C) 3	(C) 1	(C) 1	(C) 0	(C) 0	(C) 1
(D) 0	(D) 1	(D) 3	(D) 0	(D) 1	(D) 3	(D) 3
				(E) 3		
				(F) 0		

8. (A) 0	9. (A) 1	10. (A) 0	11. (A) 0	12. (A) 0	13. (A) 0
(B) 0	(B) 0	(B) 3	(B) 0	(B) 2	(B) 0
(C) 1	(C) 0	(C) 0	(C) 1	(C) 0	(C) 3
(D) 3	(D) 3		(D) 3	(D) 0	(D) 0
(E) 0	(E) 3			(E) 3	

The highest score you can get is 37 points.

If you got between 33 and 37 points, you're a master of style. You're glamorous, exciting, *never predictable.* People try to copy *you.*

If you scored between 27 and 32, you certainly have an eye for expressing the unique in you, but you don't always carry it off. With a little more courage you can learn to flaunt it!

A score of 23–26 indicates that you spend an awful lot of time seeking out models of style but don't yet know how to express your own individuality. You confuse cash with class. You're really not terribly stylish.

If you scored under 23, don't come to my house. You probably tell gross jokes. You probably put a lampshade on your head for laughs.

2

Do You Show Grace Under Pressure?

Are you cool? Not the frigid kind of cool, but the graceful-under-pressure kind? Do you fall apart when you're tense, and have clumsy and angry reactions to stress that win you no battles, allies, or friends? Or— lucky you—are you like Roseanne? Roseanne always comes through in a crunch with a sense of humor, and rises to the occasion when challenged. She has infinite class and a sense of herself. Roseanne's cool. Are you?

1. You're browsing in an elegant department store. When you turn around for a minute, your child takes the opportunity to relieve himself on the plushly carpeted floor. You say to a horrified bystander,
   A. "He's not *my* child."
   B. "Oh, look what the little devil's done now!"
   C. "Have you any tissues?"

2. You and your husband are on an airplane. There seems to be an engine problem and the pilot confirms this. You
   A. shriek a lot between short staccato gasps.
   B. say goodbye to Stanley and tell him you always loved him.
   C. hold Stanley's hand *very* tightly and count to three hundred.

D. say to Stanley, "I *told* you we should have flown Pan Am."

3. You've been working overtime with no extra pay, and your boss then asks you to take a load of work home over the weekend. You
   A. say, "Sure, no problem."
   B. smile nicely and say you're sorry but it's quite impossible.
   C. say OK but it's the last time you'll ever work overtime without extra pay.
   D. tell your boss to shove it.

4. You're serving a gorgeous filet mignon to some important clients. As you bring the roast in, the whole thing slides very neatly off the platter and onto the floor. You
   A. swiftly pick it up, dump it in the garbage, and break out the salmon.
   B. die of embarrassment, wring your hands, and take everyone out to dinner.
   C. say, "God, what a klutz I am! Luckily, I have an extra roast, identical to this one in the oven." Then you go into your kitchen, rinse the cat hairs off the roast, and put it on a different plate with a little fresh parsley—and serve it.

5. You've waited ten minutes for a parking place. It becomes vacant, but before you can park, another car darts in ahead of you. The driver gets out and begins to walk away. You stop him and
   A. explain that you were there first and the space is rightly yours.
   B. offer to crush his genitals if he doesn't move his car.
   C. promise to let the air out of his tires the moment he's gone if he doesn't move.
   D. yell "MURDERER!! POLICE!!"

6. Twice you've asked the waiter to bring ketchup for your hamburger. But the waiter is chatting with the pretty waitress and your burger is congealing. You

A. get up and get the ketchup yourself, and leave him un-tipped.
B. eat the burger without the ketchup.
C. get the ketchup and pour some on his shoe before you use it on the burger.
D. report him to the manager, leave the cold burger, and don't pay.

7. Your date is forty-five minutes late. You've bought tickets to a play you really want to see. You
   A. go to the theater, leaving him a note stating that his ticket will be at the box office.
   B. make no mention of his lateness when he arrives, and act your cool, sweet, charming self.
   C. point to the clock when he comes in. Let him know how furious you are at his uncaring attitude.

8. After the gas station has installed a new battery, your car doesn't start the next day. Your neighbor checks it out and tells you that the supposedly new battery is a used one. You
   A. firebomb the gas station.
   B. change to another gas station.
   C. threaten to sue if a new battery is not installed in twenty minutes.
   D. write an angry letter to the manager of the gas station, and call the Better Business Bureau to report him.

9. You run into a friend while checking into a motel with a man who is *not* your husband. It's embarrassing. You
   A. say you're researching an article on infidelity.
   B. wink.
   C. introduce her to your lover and explain nothing.
   D. take her aside and offer her $150 if she keeps her mouth shut.
   E. act dazed and tell her you can't remember how you got there.

10. Your best friend asks to borrow the python pocketbook that you really *hate* to loan. You

A. say OK if you can borrow her white Ultrasuede skirt (which you know she has just bought).

B. say no, you *love* your python pocketbook and know you'd both hate it if something happened to it.

C. say OK but death will come to her if she mars it.

ANSWERS AND ANALYSIS

1. *C* is the coolest response—even if you'd really like to disown the kid.

2. *C* is the most graceful way to sit out the tension. An *A* response indicates a hysteric, a *B* response indicates a melodramatic pessimist, and *D* indicates a pain-in-the-ass nag.

3. *B* is cool because she respects her own needs but knows how to be assertive without being nasty. *A* is a self-denying person who thinks it's cool to be a martyr. *C* represents crankiness, not grace under pressure, and *D* indicates a person who will soon be jobless.

4. Oh, yes—*C* is *marvelously* cool.

5. This is a toughie, but it seems that *A* is the only really cool response—even though it may not work. Still, you don't have to win everything: Really cool people can take failure without falling apart. *B* and *C* are really rather violent and may even land you in court. *D* is definitely *not* a display of grace under pressure.

6. *A* is solid coolness. *B* will leave you frustrated and unsatisfied. *C* could relieve your irritation, but it's pretty uncool behavior. *D* won't get you what you came in for: a hamburger with ketchup.

7. *A* is the smartest, most cool thing to do. *B* is self-denying, and *C* vents tension but is fruitless because you've missed the show, dummy.

8. *C* is direct and cool and probably will produce a new battery instantly. *B* is not grace under pressure because you're avoiding the issue. *D* will take time and cause you more

irritation because the Better Business Bureau will probably put you on hold with Muzak playing. *A,* while effective, is not displaying grace under pressure.

9. *A* seems to be the most sophisticated and *possible* excuse. *B* is schmuckey. *C* doesn't get you off the hook, although it does display a certain dignity—OK, OK: I'll accept *C* as correct also. *D* is desperate, not cool, and *E* would be hard to pull off.

10. *C* seems best to represent grace under pressure. Sometimes you have to do what in your heart of hearts you don't *want* to do. *A* is a sneaky, sour way of saying yes, and *B* is just not very friendly *or* cool.

SCORING

Give yourself 4 points for every correct response.

If you scored from 32 to 40 points, you know how to handle tension and minor embarrassments with aplomb. You don't let irritations drive you up the wall; instead you're probably a cool cat with a sense of humor whose life is a challenge instead of a pressure cooker. Congratulations!

A score of 24-28 indicates a person who can *generally* react with grace instead of blowing a fuse at life's little tensions. Still, you sometimes are a pushover for others, which makes you seethe inside more than you'd like.

A score of 16-20 should tell you that you have a very tough time in a crunch. You need to learn to relax and look at life with more humor and equanimity. Take a course in yoga. Take a vacation. Take it easy.

If you scored under 16, take your blood pressure. It's very high.

3

Are You a Spontaneous Person?

Everyone knows someone like her. She's the essence of spontaneity. She's impulsive, original, uncontrived. Life, for her, does not have to be wrapped up with a big pink ribbon that says *permanent.* Instead she takes her days as they joyfully unfold. She's not a cliché. Although she's not careless, she knows the value of living on the edge once in a while instead of forever playing it safe. She doesn't need endless promises, commitments, bindings. She lives in the moment, in the *here-and-now,* and she doesn't waste precious years stewing about the future.

Everyone knows someone like her—and everyone is secretly just a little jealous of her. She's a free spirit. Is she you?

In the following quiz, choose the most honest answer for you. Then check the analysis that follows to see how spontaneous you really are.

1. You're on the midnight Orient Express, chugging your way to Istanbul. There's a knock on the door of your stateroom, and opening it a crack you see it's the dark, incredibly virile-looking gentleman who sat across from you at dinner. You

A. report him to the conductor.

B. open the door wider and pull him into your room.

C. whisper that you'll meet him in the bar car in ten minutes.

D. slam the door so quickly, he barely gets his virility out of the way.

2. You have to give a wedding present to your friend. You choose

A. a Mister Coffee.

B. a Mister Peanut-Butter Maker.

C. a Mister Sushi.

D. a Mister Pasta Maker.

E. a wine-and-fruit delivery every month for a year.

F. a casserole dish.

3. You win a free weekend in London. You

A. go.

B. pack your toilet-seat covers, your Lomotil, your bottled water, and go.

C. cash the tickets in and buy yourself municipal bonds.

D. talk your friend into going with you to share the experience.

E. go because it's free, but you are *very* nervous about all that violence reported in London.

4. On your birthday you

A. are always uncomfortable because it reminds you that you're a year closer to death.

B. always treat yourself to an expensive and extravagant present on your birthday.

C. always feel a little exhilarated.

D. always get a big pimple.

5. You feel unusually sensual. The time is perfect for a love affair. You

A. go on a diet, take makeup lessons, and arrange for a cruise where you'll meet some great men.

B. go bar hopping (the nicest bars, of course).

C. call that hazel-eyed guy in advertising (you always

thought he was aloof but *so* interesting) and ask him for dinner.

D. masturbate.

6. You've never been to an orgy, a murder trial, or a political rally. Your new boyfriend, a reporter, is assigned to cover all three events in one day. He asks you to come along for the ride. You say

A. *no.* Orgies are antiwoman, political rallies can be dangerous, and murder trials are depressing. Besides, you have a dentist appointment that day.

B. *terrific!* It has to be fascinating if nothing else.

C. *maybe.* You'll let him know after you think about it.

D. *disgusting.* What would you do at the orgy? What kind of a woman does he think you are anyway? What's more, you'd probably be bored at the rally, ditto at the murder trial.

7. A fabulous business opportunity has just been offered you. It doesn't pay as much as you're now making, and it might last only for a year, but it involves travel, intrigue, and enchanting people. If you take it, you'll probably lose your tenure at your uninspiring but steady job. You

A. tell yourself you'd be stupidly impetuous to lose everything for one exciting year.

B. go home and eat some linguini, a Chunky candy bar, and an avocado.

C. discuss the problem with your mother and your ex-husband.

D. jump at the chance!

E. masturbate to *excess.*

8. After an argument with your man, you

A. have suicidal thoughts.

B. have homicidal thoughts.

C. insist upon talking out your differences then and there.

D. withdraw emotionally, bottle up your frustration— and then, probably, explode about some unimportant thing.

E. refuse to make love.

F. make love nonstop.

9. You arrive home. The phone is ringing, but it stops before you can answer it. You would probably
   A. forget about it in a second and go on with your life.
   B. call up your good friends and ask, "Did you just call me?"
   C. assume it was someone calling to tell you your mother has had a stroke.
   D. feel relieved you missed the call because it was probably someone who would have upset your plans anyway.

10. When do you usually grab your lover for a quick hug or cute genital caress?
    A. when *he* seems to need affection
    B. when you appreciate something he's done for you
    C. when he's just too delicious to resist
    D. when he dresses up in your high heels and stockings

11. You would describe your women friends, for the most part, as
    A. catty and untrustworthy but rich and beautiful.
    B. pleasant but boring, kind, and predictable.
    C. original, fun, but not always there for you.
    D. totally loyal, profound.
    E. Lithuanians.

12. What's the most appealing word? (Answer quickly without pondering.)
    A. immortality
    B. dependability
    C. impulsive
    D. logical
    E. gombroon

13. You're on a desert island. You can choose one of these five undesirable types with whom to be shipwrecked. Is he
    A. a mama's boy?

    B. a gambler?
    C. a whiner?
    D. a jealous lover?
    E. an advertising executive?

14. What you like best about your dog is her or his
    A. cute, wet nose.
    B. protectiveness.
    C. need for you.
    D. independence.
    E. constipation.

15. Being spontaneous means you have no fetishes. However, if you *did* have one, it would
    A. have something to do with airplanes.
    B. have something to do with feet.
    C. have something to do with teddies and blankies.
    D. have something to do with cleanliness.

ANSWERS AND ANALYSIS

1. *C* is the wonderfully impulsive thing to do. *B* is daring but also ditzy because you need at least a little conversation to make sure he's not the virile escaped loony. *A* is a loser, *D* a sadist.

2. *E* shows originality and free thinking. The others show a predictable, boring mentality—*yes, even the Mister Sushi.*

3. *A* is your answer. *D* needs a support section before she'll take a chance, *B* could use a portable internist, *C* could use some imagination, and *E* is a fearful person who always looks behind rather than ahead.

4. *C* really likes herself and her impulsiveness. *A* counts years instead of precious moments. Why does *B* have to wait for her birthday to treat herself? *D*'s skin reacts to her up-tightness.

5. *C* makes good sense. *A* is so calculating she doesn't know the meaning of spontaneity. *B* is hoping someone will like her instead of making a quick choice of someone *she* likes.

And *D*—well, I would never knock something that makes you feel nice, but it's a little lonely having a love affair with yourself.

6. Of course you chose *B*! *A* is a pedestrian, dull woman, *C* is a never-can-make-up-her-mind casualty, *D* is *not* going to be voted Queen of Fun, this year.

7. *D* says do it! Give life a chance! *A* will be stuck with dullness all her life; *B* puts off decisions, although the Chunky bar usually can solve a lot of dilemmas; and *C* needs direction, not free space, in which to revel.

8. *C* is what a spontaneous person would need for survival. *A* and *B* overreact, *D* is not a whole lot of fun, *E* better think about why she uses her body as a punishment, and *F* ought to think about why she uses her body as a reward for peacemaking.

9. *A* is what a free spirit would do. *B* is a nervous wretch, *C* is the author of this quiz, *D* is a suspicious, negative personality.

10. *C* indicates an impulsive personality. *B* gives hugs as calculated rewards for niceness, *A* is a self-depriving person, and *D* admires kinky behavior.

11. *C* makes sense. A spontaneous person would probably not be likely to look to *A* or *B* for meaningful friendship, and *D* is also not a very satisfying pal for her. *E* is *silly* and *such a dumb choice* that if you made it you lose *double* points! (Unless you're a native Lithuanian, in which case give yourself full credit.)

12. *C* is the word which would most likely attract a truly spontaneous person, unlike zestless *B* or *D*. *A* has very little meaning for one who lives for and in the moment. *E, gombroon?* You like that word? Yecch.

13. *B*, the gambler, would be most likely to make the long days interesting. *A* would be a terrible pain in the ass, *C* would require a gag to shut him up, and *D* would need constant reassurance that you weren't thinking of someone else. If you were shipwrecked with *E* and had to listen to stuff like "Our karma was bad," "This will be an experiential togetherness," and "Ciao," you'd be better off swimming across the ocean.

14. *D* would be an admirable trait to a truly spontaneous person. Choosing *C* might imply respect for subservience, *B* respect for a guardian, and *A* respect for a toy. Don't knock *E* if you live in a place where you have to pooper-scoop.

15. Festishism consists of revering an object which you believe to have magical or irresistible qualities. If you chose *A* you probably have an attraction toward flight, freedom, and adventure. *B* would entail a love for what *smells*—not exactly a free-spirited characteristic; *C* would suggest a love for one's own childhood—kind of a confining concept; and *D,* who needs pristine purity, is definitely repressed.

SCORING

Give yourself 10 points for every correct answer.

If you scored 120–150 points, you're a joyful, spontaneous creature, as exciting as you are excited, living your life to the fullest and not, as T.S. Eliot suggested, measuring it out in coffee spoons.

If you scored 90–110, you're fairly adept at "seizing the moment," but still let too many of those moments slip by as you hesitate or fret about consequences. Relax, enjoy! Celebrate your ability to say *yes* to life!

If you scored 70–80, you create too many regrets for yourself. You've been known to make a daring move on rare occasions, but you drown your capacity for spontaneity in fears.

If you scored under 70, better get thee to a nunnery. You probably follow directions well and even work and play well with others, but your days are formulas that are never broken by inventiveness or surprise. *Let go!*

4

Do You Have
Street Smarts?

Street smarts are nothing
more than good old common sense. You can have a Ph.D.
from Yale and still be so light in the commonsense department that you can't find your way home in a snowstorm. On
the other hand, there's someone like Blanche. She could
never afford to go to college, but because she can make quick,
workable judgments and has shrewd street smarts, she can get
along in Paris and Tahiti as well as her own hometown. She's
a winner in her career and personal life—without the diploma.
Street smarts are great smarts to have. They protect you from
trickery, wasted time, and danger, and allow you to open up to
life—safely. Everyone thinks Blanche just lucks out all the
time, but it's not just luck—it's street smarts. Test yourself to
see if you have them.

1. You're in your car, stopped at a red light in a very lonely
   section of town. Two men approach the car and begin to
   make sexual innuendos. You
   A. quietly but firmly explain that you don't like that kind
      of talk.
   B. roll up the window and ignore them.
   C. floor the gas, pass the red light, and get out of there.
   D. shoot them.

2. A peddler on the street, acting furtive, offers you a gorgeous, gold (stamped "14-karat") bracelet for $20. You
   A. grab it! It's probably stolen merchandise and he needs to get rid of it quickly; either that or he doesn't know its value.
   B. bargain him down to $15. If he's selling "hot" merchandise, you ought to get an even bigger bargain.
   C. walk away; the bracelet is no bargain.
   D. give him a little lecture on morality.

3. When buying a new car, you can realistically expect to pay
   A. the sticker price.
   B. more than the sticker price.
   C. less than the sticker price.

4. You're alone in a subway car. A drunken, leering man gets on at the next stop. You
   A. turn briskly and walk to the center car in search of the conductor.
   B. pull the emergency brake.
   C. ignore the man, not even making eye contact.
   D. shout, "Help!"
   E. shoot him.

5. You're being interviewed for a new job. The boss asks you, "What's your greatest flaw?" You answer,
   A. "I'm a nymphomaniac."
   B. "I'm an incurable perfectionist."
   C. "Procrastination."
   D. "Sloppiness."

6. A wonderful "special" is advertised in the newspaper. When you get there, the salesman says he's out of the merchandise but has a much better model that's a bit more expensive. You
   A. are the victim of a supply-and-demand situation.
   B. are the victim of a bait-and-switch ploy.
   C. are appreciative of his thoughtfulness and buy the better merchandise.
   D. punch him in the nose.

7. At a party, you meet a charming Harvard graduate who offers you a safe way to double your money fast. You
   A. give him $5000 of your savings. It's worth a shot to take the advice of someone so bright, and besides he's a friend of your host.
   B. see if anyone famous or influential has invested with him. If they have, take him up on the offer. What makes you smarter than they?
   C. go check out the hors d'oeuvres. This guy's bad news.

8. A brand-new appliance breaks. You've lost the warranty and the manager refuses to fix it. You
   A. write the manager an angry letter and threaten to sue him.
   B. accept the results of your carelessness and have the appliance fixed at your own expense.
   C. call the president of the company and ask him to do something.
   D. throw the appliance through the store window.

9. Whom do you most admire?
   A. Marilyn Monroe
   B. Joan of Arc
   C. Gloria Steinem

10. You're approaching a tollbooth in your car. The lines of traffic are murder. You invariably
    A. honk a lot.
    B. get in the exact-change lane.
    C. get in the extreme-right-hand lane with all the trucks.
    D. pick your nose.

11. You're eating alone in a restaurant, and someone at a table nearby is staring at you. You
    A. lean over and say, "Do I know you?"
    B. ask the waiter to eject him from the restaurant.
    C. change your seat so you face totally away from him.
    D. put a paper bag over your head.

12. In a crowded bus, you suddenly feel a hand slither into your purse. You

A. hold it.

B. scream, shriek, and kick the hand in the shins.

C. freeze. (Losing your wallet is better than losing your life.)

13. A cosmetics set arrives in the mail with a letter that asks you either to make a $5 donation or to return the item. You didn't order it and don't want it. You

A. return it to the manufacturer.

B. keep it or throw it away without sending any money.

C. give the donation rather than going to the bother of returning it.

14. Which statement is true?

A. Never buy any merchandise from street merchants. It's bound to be of poor quality.

B. In a foreign country, always ask the cabdriver how much the ride will be *before* you get in the cab if you don't want to be cheated.

C. Women are easy pawns for men. Never believe a man who flatters you or wants to sell you something soon after you meet.

15. Your boyfriend Ronald has a cute bottom. He has just gotten a job with an older woman lawyer as a paralegal. He needs the work, but every time he bends over his word processor, she manages to walk past and stroke that bottom. He doesn't want to lose the job but he feels used. He should

A. explain that men hate being sex objects as much as women do.

B. tell her she reminds him of his mother who also loves his bottom.

C. grab her wrist and tell her to just cut it out.

D. stroke *her* bottom.

E. have a long talk with her about Proust.

ANSWERS AND ANALYSIS

1. *C* is the answer. It's better to break a law than risk your safety. Only a cockeyed optimist would think that *A* would work; *B* is about as effective as an ostrich hiding its head in the sand; and *D* is somewhat of an overreaction.

2. *C* is the response of a street-smart person, who would know that it's easy to stamp "14-karat" on anything. One of the biggest games in town, of late, is *pretending* to have stolen merchandise so that less-than-honest buyers will think they've found a bargain.

3. *C* is correct. Competitive tactics always dictate that a good car salesman offer you "a little something off." A street-smart person would never pay the asking price for a new car.

4. *A* makes the most sense. *B* is dramatic but dopey; *C* would accomplish very little; *D* is dumb because there's no one else around; and if you chose *E* again, you *really* have a problem with overreacting.

5. *B* is the answer a street-smart person would offer. It's one a boss would like to hear, because it says your worst flaw is a business asset. Anyone who chose *A, C,* or *D* really needs a course in common sense.

6. *B* is the right answer here. A woman with street smarts would know she has been lured in with false promises and would never make a purchase in that store.

7. *C* is the *only* answer. An *A* or *B* answer indicates someone with street dumbs.

8. *C* would almost surely work. Going to the top, to the head of even the most famous companies is what a street-smart person knows is possible. General Motors really does answer the telephone.

9. A street-smart woman would probably most admire someone like *C,* Gloria Steinem, who teaches other women how to get what's rightfully theirs. Joan of Arc (*B*) was very nice and brave and she died for her ideals, but she died. Idealistic, yes; street smart, no. And Marilyn Monroe (*A*) was a

woman who, although a symbol of sexuality, could never protect herself against the world's hurts—not someone a street-smart woman would admire.

10. *C,* believe it or not. Despite the length of the trucks' line, it generally moves through the tollbooths faster, because there are fewer trucks than cars: one truck for every two or three cars, typically. Exact change lanes, studies find, are often, perversely, the slowest moving and longest.

11. Common sense says *C* is the only answer.

12. *B* is street-smartest. Pickpockets are generally not murderers, and your life is not in danger here, just your wallet. If you chose *A,* you are abnormally lonely, better call a dating service.

13. *B* is correct. You have no obligation to return or pay for unordered merchandise. Street-smart people won't be taken in by this common ruse.

14. *No* statement here is true. Give yourself points if you rejected *every* generality. Street-wise people are never taken in by glittering generality.

15. *A* makes good street sense. *B* will get him back on the street job hunting, *C* is macho-stupido, *D* is for dumb, and *E* is irrelevant.

SCORING

Each correct answer is worth 10 points.

If you scored from *120 to 150 points,* you are absolute dynamite in the commonsense department. You're quick-witted without being rash, and you cope as well with emergencies as with everyday decisions. You're sensitive to trickery, and understand what is real danger and what is just taking a calculated risk. You can survive wonderfully well in almost any environment, and your street smarts make you an admired person whose judgments are always respected.

If you scored from 90 to 110, you often are correct in your appraisal of situations, but false veneers, promises, and personalities tend to trip you up just a little more than you like.

Practise stepping back and thinking through a situation, eventually you will be able automatically to assess the street-smart move.

If you scored from 70 to 80, you really make too many rash and unwise decisions. More often than not, you're tricked or trapped into making a move that has negative implications for you. You're gullible, and you're victimized too often, even though you may be pretty cute. Take time to think before you blurt out yes or no.

If you scored under 70, you not only do not have street smarts but shouldn't even go out on the street without taking along an advisor.

5

Are You Your Own Worst Enemy?

Are you your own worst enemy? Do you cling to destructive romances, going-nowhere jobs, and make-no-one-happy relationships?

Too many of us complain about bad luck or missed opportunities when in fact it is our own self-defeating attitudes and actions that doom us to failure. It's no great cause for alarm if you occasionally sabotage your own success because you're thinking negatively or are perhaps fearful of a particular achievement, but if you're in a continual *pattern* of self-destructive behavior you need to reassess your motives—you need help.

Take this short quiz to see whether you have been regularly denying yourself success, and whether your unhappiness is actually self-induced.

1. What's a typical behavior pattern for you?
   A. bingeing on junk food when depressed
   B. changing lovers when your current lover disappoints you greatly
   C. mellowing out with pot (or tranquilizers or whatever) when things get hairy
   D. kicking and screaming when angry

2. Your host asks you which you'd prefer—red or white wine. You say,
   A. "Whatever is easiest."
   B. "White *and* red."
   C. "Rosé."
   D. "Wine gives me a headache."
   E. either "White" or "Red."

3. Your husband (or lover) has confessed to having an affair with someone else. "Just give me time to break it off," he asks. "I need time to break it gently." You
   A. give him approximately five minutes.
   B. arrange to have him murdered.
   C. are very understanding, even though you're heartbroken. Knowing that it'll blow over eventually, you give him no ultimatum.
   D. insist on a divorce (or breakup) immediately. You can never trust him again.

4. Your father died a year ago and your loving (but joyless and judgmental mother) says she hates living alone. You
   A. are a good daughter, if nothing else, and you ask her to move in with you.
   B. fix her up with someone.
   C. arrange for her to have a live-in companion and share the expense with her.
   D. tell her that everyone is responsible for her own happiness and you have your own problems.

5. Have you ever stopped to ask yourself why in the world you are involved in the job you have now?
   A. yes
   B. no

6. It's the big office party. You tell a joke on yourself and the punch line makes you seem as if
   A. you're a victim of your own easygoing ways.
   B. everyone is picking on you unfairly.
   C. you're defeated but adorable.
   D. you're an incurable botcher-up.

7. You're about to make a serious commitment to a man. This is how you feel about him:
   A. He's got big problems, sure, but no one is perfect and a reasonable person ought to compromise.
   B. He's very nice, although he's not too handsome—then again, you're not the prettiest woman in the world.
   C. You and he have the most blazing, infuriating battles, but the heartache soon disappears when you passionately make up.
   D. You can't imagine a life without him.
   E. So he'll wear a paper bag on his head when you bring him home to your parents.

8. Do you try to correct the small external details in life that nevertheless get you nervous or uptight (stuff like hems hanging down, leaky pens, creaking doors, a mediocre butcher)?
   A. You make an effort to try to live with minor annoyances rather than let them drive you crazy.
   B. You never seem to find time for them.
   C. You ignore them, successfully.
   D. You usually try to remove such irritants.

9. When things don't work out, you find yourself saying something like
   A. "Everything I touch turns sour."
   B. "No wonder. I surely deserved this."
   C. "Shit!"

10. Your husband or lover is untrustworthy, poverty stricken, immature, and demanding; still, you love him. Looking into the future, you see
    A. nothing changed: the two of you together, just like now.
    B. everything changed. You plan to leave him.
    C. everything changed. You know you'll work it out together.
    D. a big rock falling from the sky onto his head.

ANSWERS AND ANALYSIS

1. *D* is the only healthy pattern. It is as self-destructive and addictive to binge on junk food and lovers as on drugs.

2. *D* or *E* are the best. *A* says you consider yourself too undeserving to have a choice, *B* is greedy and bound to make you seem undesirable to your host, a *C* choice says that you are almost never satisfied with what is available. If you chose any of the last three, you are not being good to yourself.

3. *A* is probably the most well-adjusted response, even though, I confess, my insecurities would probably lead me to choose *D*—and thereby lose a possibly terrific person who had simply made a mistake. *B* is a mild overreaction which would get you into trouble. *C* is the most self-destructive thing you could do because this choice belittles your integrity and worth.

4. *C* is the choice that says you will not allow yourself to be strangled by a destructive though loving relationship (*A*). *B* is unrealistic, and *D* is just plain mean.

5. You may have questions about your job, but you really shouldn't be *so* doubtful that you're doing the right thing for you. Sometimes a false sense of ambition that's not really *you,* as well as others' prodding, can land you in a position where you are a victim either of overreach or of under-challenge. It is very self-defeating to put yourself in a work situation that makes you wonder why you're there.

6. *C* is the only choice that doesn't have you undermining yourself in public—always a destructive act.

7. *D* is the only answer that says you're not your own enemy. In a love relationship you should *never* compromise or settle on anyone of whom you're ashamed, with whom you fight inordinately, or who is seriously troubled. If you think so little of yourself that you feel you must take whatever you can get, get help—fast!—before you do real damage to your life and end up trapped and defeated.

8. *D,* of course. If you can easily dispense with an irri-

tant and you don't, that's a sure sign of self-sabotage. You *want* to hurt yourself by these annoying little aggravations. Using up energy in stoically trying to live with stuff you can get rid of is not noble martyrdom—it's self-hurt.

9. *C* is the most rational response. Negative thinking and poor expectations of your own performance are self-fulfilling prophecies. If you think you'll fail, if you think your touch is doomed, you cannot possibly succeed. Such an attitude is almost destined to bring you down, no matter how talented you are.

10. *B* is the only route a self-liking person would choose. The man in your life is bad news, and clinging to a bad relationship is the most dangerous form of being an enemy to yourself. It's suicidal, in a way, to stick around for more of the same (*A*) or to hope unrealistically that miracles can make him change (*C*). If you chose *D,* just think what your psyche is trying to tell you about how you *really* feel about such a destructive romance.

SCORING

Give yourself 10 points for every *self-affirming* answer.

If you scored between 90 and 100 points, you're your own best friend. You are in control of your life, have realistic and positive expectations, and operate on the theory that *you count* and are valuable. You do not indulge in tactics that will stalemate your happiness, because you like success and don't fear it. You are independent and give off vibrations that say, I am comfortable with success and winning and love.

If you scored between 70 and 80, you are generally supportive of yourself, but too often find yourself going for options that cannot succeed. Perhaps at those times you are subconsciously punishing yourself by orchestrating defeats. However, for the most part you choose people and situations that will bring you satisfaction and happiness. Don't be afraid to make a stand and to call the shots in your life: You are basically out for your own good and know how to achieve it.

If you scored between 40 and 60, stop short and take stock of where you're going! Your projects and relationships may be failing because you are writing a script that spells failure. You make judgments that are self-destructive too often for your failures to be mere accidents. Look honestly into yourself: Are you angry at yourself? Does your need to please, to be a "good girl," get in the way of your personal growth? Are you sabotaging happiness?

If you scored under 40, perhaps you really are unworthy: Hit yourself again!

6

Is Your Health
in Jeopardy?

Caught up in the hustle and bustle of finding success in career and personal life, we often ignore our body's needs. We carelessly concentrate our attention on what seem more pressing priorities than health. And when we do that we open the door to the development of cardiac, respiratory, and gastrointestinal disorders, not to mention the crippling anxiety that a friend of mine calls "nerbs."

The fact is that no matter how busy you are, you should take time out to consider your present and future health. Certain diets, drugs, habits, and stresses may be irrevocably sabotaging your body. Your mother was right: "If you don't have your health," she said—remember?—"nothing else counts." Even finding the "G spot" won't mean a thing.

Take this quiz to see if you're taking care of your health—physically *and* mentally.

1. You have these particular signs of distress at least three times a week:
   A. chronic diarrhea or constipation
   B. a whole lot of belching
   C. dizzy spells
   D. horniness
   E. shortness of breath

2. You have these particular signs of stress at least three times a week: You
   A. feel like you want to cry but can't.
   B. find yourself grinding your teeth.
   C. have a definite lack of interest in sex.
   D. have a feeling of mild panic.
   E. feel like you need to escape something or someone.
   F. feel irritable.
   G. can't stop thinking of your problems.

3. When you can't sleep, you
   A. masturbate.
   B. take a Valium or sleeping pill.
   C. make a phony phone call.
   D. do something else, such as reading or writing a letter.
   E. eat.

4. How many of these statements are true for you?
   A. "I hardly ever give myself a breast examination. I'm just too squeamish and afraid I'll find something."
   B. "I'm pretty impatient with pokey drivers. I almost always exceed a speed limit."
   C. "I smoke—all kinds of glorious things."
   D. "I'm ugly and worthless."
   E. "I often drink alone."

5. Answer true or false:
   A. "Pastrami will do me in one day."
   B. "Taking vitamin pills is unnecessary if I eat a balanced diet."
   C. "I'm a junk-food junkie with a diet composed mainly of stuff like tacos, pizza, cookies, or Chunky candy bars.
   D. "I daily eat a substantial amount of salt or red meat."
   E. "I have had one of these diseases this year: beriberi, rickets, scurvy, anemia, pellagra, crabs."

6. Which is true about your dieting habits?
   A. You tend to go on yo-yo diets (lose ten pounds, gain eleven, lose ten, gain eleven, and so on).
   B. In the last six months you have gone on at least three of these diets: the Scarsdale Diet, Beverly Hills Diet,

Last Chance Diet, The Grapefruit or Ice Cream or Watermelon Diet.

   C. It's either fast or binge with you.

7. How many statements seem to ring true of you?
   A. "I usually seem to set impossibly high goals for myself."
   B. "I'm as cute as a button."
   C. "I get *very* hostile and angry when I lose."
   D. "I am almost always pressured for time."

8. You would rather
   A. take the stairs than the escalator or elevator.
   B. walk than take a cab or bus.
   C. exercise than lie down.
   D. none of the above.
   E. argue, take a blood test, eat a disgusting thing—*anything* but exercise!

9. Your overall picture of life is best represented by the following statement:
   A. "The future looks pretty bleak to me."
   B. "Usually I feel optimistic about the way things are going."
   C. "I feel nauseous."
   D. "They're all after me."
   E. "Life is a treadmill."
   F. "Life is a challenge."
   G. "Life is a worm."

10. You have frequent headaches. You think they may come from
    A. a brain tumor.
    B. your birth-control pill.
    C. your habit of sleeping with your head under the covers.
    D. coffee withdrawal.
    E. too much sex.
    F. eye problems.

11. Many chronic diseases like heart disease, ulcers, colitis
    A. are inherited and thus inevitable.

B. always come with age.

C. start with the suppression of symptoms you don't like to admit.

D. are incurable.

E. are punishments from God.

12. When you have a cold and fever, you most likely
   A. see a doctor.
   B. ignore them and continue your activities.
   C. consider it a life crisis.
   D. live on chicken soup, aspirin, and rest.
   E. kvetch.

13. To eliminate stress, you might very likely
   A. take a nap.
   B. take a pill.
   C. think about something else.
   D. punch something.
   E. shriek or scream.

14. When you're really very tired, you
   A. take only those stimulants that your doctor prescribed.
   B. take a nap.
   C. have a Coke, coffee, or candy bar to pep you up.
   D. use your mind and willpower to convince yourself you're not really tired.
   E. meditate.

15. "My state of health is
   A. most intelligently left up to my physicians."
   B. my own responsibility."
   C. my mother's responsibility."
   D. not worth taking too much time over, because of my youth."
   E. out of my control."

ANSWERS AND ANALYSIS

1. If you have *any* of those signs (except *D*) so regularly, your health is already threatened by stress or real physical

problems. See a doctor. Horniness is, most of us think, a sign of health which ought to be immediately gratified.

2. *F* is the only answer that's acceptable because only a clam is not irritated at least three times a week. The other stress signals are clear indications that you're in a tension danger zone. An overload of such stress can make you a prime candidate for heart or digestive trouble.

3. *A* or *D* would probably induce healthful stress release. *B* and *E* responses indicate a reliance on drugs or oral gratification through eating. A *C* response indicates that you're either slow-witted or nine years old.

4. This is the "death-wish" question. *None* of the statements indicate an attitude of good mental or physical health. If three or more statements are true for you—get help. You're not going to stay healthy for long.

5. Only *B* shows an awareness of eating right for health. The other choices indicate dietary deficiencies or overloads (except for getting crabs, which indicates poor luck).

6. If *any* of these statements are true, you're dieting your way to ill health. As regards *A*, weight loss followed by weight gain in a habitual pattern elevates serum-cholesterol levels and increases arterial fat clogging and skin sag. *B* indicates that you're a diet freak instead of a sensible eater. *C* involves extremes either of which has to be devastating to health when done regularly.

7. *B* is the only response that shows self-approval. The other answers indicate people who are prime candidates for stomach or heart trouble because of the high levels of tension they create for themselves.

8. If you answered *D* or *E,* you are not exercising enough to insure good health.

9. *Life is a worm?* If you gave this answer, you're quite odd. If you answered *B* or *F,* your mental health promotes physical health. Any other answers indicate trouble and doctors.

10. *B, C,* and *D* are the most likely possibilities and often cause headaches. Brain tumors are rare, and eye problems

also rarely cause headaches. Too much sex may give you an infection, but not a headache.

11. *C* is the only true answer. If you answered *E* you need a psychiatrist or a religious counselor.

12. *D* and *E* are sensible answers. *A* and *C* are overreactions; *B* is an underreaction.

13. *D* and *E* work nicely. *A*, *B*, and *C* don't.

14. *B* and *E* are healthful responses.

15. *B* is the attitude that has the best chance of insuring good health.

SCORING

Give yourself 10 points for every question in which you were able to pick the most health-giving responses.

If you tallied 120-150 points, you have a sophisticated awareness of what makes for good health. But you have more than that: You are in control of your stress patterns and rarely have tension overloads serious enough to undermine your body. What's more, your diet, exercise, and self-treatment habits usually combine to assure you happy, healthy days.

If you tallied 90-110, you likely have a good general-health pattern, but could probably use more common sense in daily diet and exercise habits. What's more, you need to do a little self-searching to determine how stress can be better dissipated. Do some reading on meditation, yoga, and self-massage, which often help.

A score of 70-80 says that you're really *not* coping with stress in your daily life and you ought to think about getting help if problems or tensions become overwhelming. Your physical well-being is not enough of a concern to you, and you'd better be careful! It's not too late: You *can* reconstitute a shaky health outlook into a resilient one. *Listen* to your body!

If you scored under 70 on this quiz, you have crummy health consciousness and prognosis. I hope you're very rich, which will compensate a little (no matter what they say).

7

Are You a Survivor?

Not only forest creatures live in a challenging and dangerous environment. How you face up to danger and the pressures of love and hate determine if you are indeed one of life's happy survivors. Often survival is a matter of imagination and self-confidence. People who panic cannot cope, and they spend their days in crescendos of frustration, impatience, and self-orchestrated failure. This quiz is designed to show you just how gracefully you *can* carry on in real or imaginary crisis situations. Time is of the essence in this quiz; you only have twelve minutes to complete your answers! Survival, you see, is also the ability to make quick decisions.

1. You're alone in the house; a handsome man rings your bell, says his car has broken down, and asks to use your phone. You
   A. tell him to wait a minute, go put on lipstick, and invite him in.
   B. ask for his credentials before you let him in.
   C. ask him to wait where he is while you make the call for him.

2. Back at the lodge after skiing, you notice yellowish-white spots on your foot. You remember this is a sign of frostbite. You
   A. immediately apply ice or snow to the area.
   B. rub briskly or exercise the frostbitten parts.
   C. put your foot in your date's armpits or between his thighs.
   D. threaten to sue.

3. What a cocktail party—everybody is brilliant! You, however, are in over your head, intellectually. You
   A. make yourself inconspicuous and keep your mouth shut so no one will see how inadequate you are.
   B. ask a whole lot of questions.
   C. leave.
   D. change the subject to something with which you're familiar—like the recent hysterectomy of your cat.
   E. start a big fight.

4. Stranded in the desert! The nearest town is a week's walk away. You
   A. ration your water drastically and walk briskly in the daylight hours toward your destination.
   B. walk slowly, at night.
   C. stay put and drink healthy swigs of gin until you're found.
   D. take off all those hot clothes and jog toward town at a regular pace.

5. You have just lost your job. Prospects for finding another are bleak. You
   A. check into the possibilities of becoming an entrepreneur with your own business.
   B. register with the well-known employment agencies.
   C. write a furious but brilliantly clever letter to your boss telling him what an asshole you've always thought he was, anyway.
   D. eat an awesome amount.

6. Whom do you most admire?
   A. Elvis Presley

B. Helen Keller
C. Amelia Earhart
D. Juliet and Cleopatra

7. You're shipwrecked on a desert island. Choose one of the following items which you may have:
A. a small boat
B. a sharp knife
C. a three-months' supply of food
D. an electric vibrator

8. You've been invited to a fabulous party, but it's in a terrible neighborhood. You
A. stay home where it's safe and snuggley.
B. take off without a moment's hesitation down the mugger block because you don't believe in living in fear.
C. practise your martial arts, take a police whistle, some Mace, and a knife—and walk briskly to the party.
D. stuff a hump under your blouse and paste some false drool (or work up the real stuff) on the side of your mouth, and no one will bother with you.

9. You get on an elevator and a sleazy-looking character follows you in. You press the button for your floor, he presses no button, and when you arrive at your floor he begins to follow you off. You
A. start screaming.
B. walk toward your apartment without doing any crazy thing like screaming because you could well be wrong about him.
C. ask him if he too is looking for the Syphilis Foundation.
D. get back in the elevator.

10. You're swimming from your yacht and you see a shark's fin. You
A. kick and thrash about wildly.
B. stay absolutely still.
C. swim back to the boat as quietly as possible.
D. do your bluefish imitation and fool the shark.

11. Which of the following five words most appeals to you?
    A. submission
    B. endurance
    C. disenchantment
    D. Mommy
    E. palimony

12. You would be most happy if you could eat your next meal
    A. at an exotic restaurant in Istanbul.
    B. in a favorite restaurant where the headwaiter knows your name.
    C. at your Aunt Maxine's house.
    D. in the bathtub.

13. The lover who's been sharing your home for two years says he wants more "space" because he now thinks you're kind of dull. You offer him
    A. a larger room in your apartment.
    B. a dozen reasons why everyone else thinks you're terrific.
    C. the sidewalk.
    D. a very nice stereo if he stays.
    E. a rational plan where you can both date other people and still live together.

14. It's been a *very* bad day. The pimple broke, the dog vomited on the Chinese carpet, and the Fire Maniac struck in your office building. You
    A. hide under the covers.
    B. have a stiff drink. Then another. And another. And . . .
    C. make a list of all the good things in your life and reasons why tomorrow will be a better day.

ANSWERS AND ANALYSIS

1. *C* is the only savvy answer if you wish to survive.
2. *C* will slowly warm the frozen tissue. *A* will make it worse, and *B* might injure or tear the frozen tissue. *D* won't

work because anyone who goes skiing assumes a possible case of frostbite.

3. *B* is the thing to do: You'll learn something and everyone loves to explain his or her field of expertise! Losing yourself in the woodwork (*A*) is not exactly imaginative survival. If you chose *C*, you chose failure; *D*, disgusted looks; and *E*, a bloody nose or worse.

4. *B* is definitely the sensible course. The point is to avoid dehydration by rationing your sweat and not your water. Also, slow motion will make you last longer, which is why *A* is incorrect. *C* cuts down your survival chances because alcohol contains products which must be eliminated through the kidneys—creating dehydration. If you chose *D*, you would expose yourself to the brutal sun without any protection.

5. *A* seems most creatively geared toward business survival. *B* is wrong because most job-hunting experts say that agencies are usually the last to know when the good jobs are available; advertising and networking seem to be the most effective. *C* won't do much to get you that letter of recommendation you'll need, and *D* is satisfying but not the best job-hunting survival tactic.

6. *B*, Helen Keller, is the person who would probably appeal most to a survivor, because she survived against all odds. Drug-besotted Presley (*A*) did not and neither did lost-in-the-stars Earhart (*C*). Juliet and Cleopatra (*D*) were romantic but definitely suicidal.

7. *B* makes the most sense for survival because a knife can create shelter, fishing materials, and protection. A small boat (*A*) would mean taking a big chance in an open sea, and *C* would not do you any good in the fourth month. A vibrator (*D*) is kinky and comforting but silly unless you've landed on an island with electricity—say Bermuda.

8. *C* sounds like a survivor to me! *A* plays it boringly safe—survivors have to take *some* risks to have a colorful life. *B* needs a talk from her mother. No one will bother with *D* at the party either.

9. *A* uses common sense; she'll worry about hurting someone's feelings later. *B* is probably *right* about the sleazy-

looking character if she is following her instincts—survivors learn to trust them. If you chose *C,* you're witty but you'll probably get your wallet lifted or worse. *D* is a dead duck.

10. *C* makes good survival sense, because sharks love *A.* Juicy bluefish (*D*) are their favorite brunch. As for *B,* it's kind of hard to stay absolutely still in the ocean.

11. A survivor would find *B* an attractive concept. *A* and *C* are loser words. *D* is sweet but sick if you're over 18. But *E,* palimony—well, hmmmm, maybe it also would indicate a survivor instinct. Yes, it definitely would . . . Count it correct, along with *B.*

12. *A* is correct: Most survivors love to roam, explore, and try out new stuff so they can practise their survival skills.

13. *C* is the healthiest self-survival choice. *A, B,* and *D* are desperate measures. *E,* my child, just would never work.

14. *A,* believe it or not, is the correct response. Every true survivor knows that even survivors need to hide in a warm place every once in a while. *B* will make you nauseous. If you chose *C,* that makes *me* nauseous because you're too much of a Pollyanna to be true.

SCORING

Each correct response is worth 10 points.

If you scored between 120 and 140 points, you're a winner! Very little in life can flatten you, because you are naturally able to cope with danger, emotional crises, and personal dilemmas. Your survival instincts are intact!

If you scored between 90 and 110, your survival instincts need a bit of sharpening up. You manage to end up on top of most situations, but too often your common sense goes blooey when stress situations crop up.

If you scored between 70 and 90, you are in great danger of folding when a really crucial survival situation arises. Practise up on quick thinking—fast!

Anyone who scored under 70 ought to stay inside a padded cage.

8

How Far Have You Come in Ten Years?

A lot of mind stretching and body freeing has gone on in the last ten years, but many have not noticed the revolution at hand. Have you ever just stopped for a moment to chart your progress over the last year or five years or ten years? Have you come a long way, or are you still stuck in dated values and victories? Take this quiz to find out.

1. Ten years ago, you would have been more than satisfied with simply getting a good job. Today, you
   A. make sure that *no one* (man or woman) gets paid more for doing the same job.
   B. need to be the boss.
   C. sleep with the boss.
   D. have learned to steal from the boss (just like the others).

2. Ten years ago, you fantasized about finding the perfect man. Today, you
   A. are still looking.
   B. have given up looking.
   C. are looking for ways to make yourself more perfect.
   D. are looking for the perfect woman.

3. Ten years ago, you mostly rested in your free time. Today you
   A. exercise daily.
   B. still hyperventilate when you climb a flight of stairs.
   C. plan to start jogging or swimming next Purim.
   D. mostly have carnal relations in your free time.

4. Ten years ago, you would have asked your date to order a pink lady for you when you went to a bar. Today you
   A. order your regular shot of scotch with a beer chaser.
   B. feel free not to order alcohol at all, if that's your pleasure.
   C. would never go to a bar. It's too tacky and low class.
   D. often take your own clients or friends out for a sociable drink (and find it comfortable to pick up the check, also).

5. Ten years ago, you worried about the war in Vietnam. Today you're worried about
   A. gum disease.
   B. the dangers of nuclear power plants.
   C. not finding a man who wants to marry you.
   D. not finding your G spot.

6. Ten years ago, you were living hand-to-mouth. Today you
   A. are deeply in debt.
   B. live in palatial splendor.
   C. find tax shelters appealing.
   D. are not rich but have a good chance of getting rich.
   E. shop with food stamps.

7. Ten years ago, you listened to your mother. Today, you listen to
   A. your husband.
   B. your lover.
   C. your inner voice.
   D. a different drummer.
   E. Heloise.

8. Ten years ago, your interests were narrowly focused. Today you're interested primarily in

    A. revenge.

    B. eating.

    C. screwing.

    D. building an empire.

    E. building relationships.

9. Ten years ago, you thought herpes was something green that came in a pod and grew in a garden. Today you
   A. have it.
   B. are much more sexually selective.
   C. are fearful about any new sexual relationships.

10. Ten years ago, you could count four people who really admired you. Today you
    A. think there are three.
    B. think that you are greatly admired by many.
    C. are not worried about being admired as long as you're loved.
    D. think admiration's a crock. It's making money that counts in this world.

11. When you look in the mirror you see
    A. the abominable snowman.
    B. perfection.
    C. a person who has developed at least one brand-new *major* interest in the last year or so.
    D. a person steeped in nostalgia for the past.
    E. fingerprints.

12. When thinking about the *next* ten years and romantic love and sexuality, you feel
    A. depressed.
    B. that kind of thing will undoubtedly fade as companionship and security become more relevant.
    C. that you can expect even more romantic passion as the years pass.
    D. disgusted at the thought of all that filth after forty.
    E. sure you'll be content with your tatting.

ANSWERS AND ANALYSIS

1. Clearly, *A* or *B* are the answers that point to the most progress. *C* is clever only if you have married the boss. *D* is a step backward.

2. *C* is the only response that connotes growth. Finding perfection in others doesn't mean beans in terms of personal victory.

3. *A* is great. And don't knock *D*, which is the best exercise around.

4. *B* or *D* represents progress. *A* represents a truck driver. *C* represents a dolt.

5. *B* shows a continuing pattern of social consciousness. *A* shows deterioration instead of progress, *C* shows a dependent mentality, and *D* is silly.

6. *C* and *D* are equal signs of progress and *B* is super. *A* and *E* tell you that you haven't developed all that much business acuity in the last ten years.

7. *C* is the only answer that says you've come a long way. Grown-ups shouldn't listen to anyone's conscience but their own.

8. *E* shows the most healthy progress, but I'll accept *D* which sounds like fun as well.

9. *B* is the ten-year winner here.

10. If you chose *B*, you've come a long way; *A*, it's a pity for you; *C*, you're unrealistic—true love *requires* admiration; *D*, you're rich but unpopular—not an awful lot of progress, unless you're Richard Nixon.

11. *C* is the person who has come furthest. *A* hates herself, *B* thinks she can go no further, *D* is sad, and *E* sees only fogging imperfections.

12. If you chose *C* you're a positive thinker. What you really expect, you'll probably get.

SCORING

Each correct response is worth 10 points.

If you scored from 110 to 120 points, congratulations! You're a doing, achieving person who moves through her days with zest. Yours is not a static world but a world of progress. The next ten years should follow this pattern of personal growth, mobility, and joie de vivre.

If you racked up 80 to 100 points, you're on a moving track, but it's a bit *slow* moving. Change is the name of your personal game, but you tend to take too few risks to have truly satisfying advancement. Reevaluate your goals and the steps you take to win them.

If your score is 60 to 70 points, you're fatally set in your ways. You need to take chances, try new things, make moves to keep your personality and life fluid. You may take steps forward, but they are too few and too small; as George Burns once said, "If you take little steps, you don't get anywhere."

And if you only scored under 60 points, pinch yourself to see if you're still breathing. An immovable object like you is not a barrel of laughs at a party.

YOU
and How You Play
with Others

9

How Well Do You
Deal with Criticism?

To some people, criticism is a punch in the face. They simply collapse with anger, frustration, or self-disgust if anyone says they've done wrong. Other people, in contrast, can roll with the punch. They listen to the criticism, determine if there is validity to the unfavorable judgment, and, if there is, are able to accept it and learn from it. They are secure enough to do this and also to recognize unfair criticism and either ignore or counter it—whichever is to their advantage.

Do you crumble at the first sign of a raised eyebrow? Or can you deal with people who put you down? The following quiz will show how secure you are. The rules are simple: Choose your most honest, instant response—not the response you'd *like* to have.

1. When someone criticizes you, your instinctive feeling is to
   A. cripple him or her.
   B. assume he or she is very jealous of you.
   C. defend yourself.
   D. check out the criticism to see if it has any validity.

2. Social scientists have discovered that most working

women take criticism more poorly than most working men. A likely reason for this is that

A. they're more sensitive by nature.
B. they have grown up believing that criticism implies *they* are deficient personally, not that they are doing a deficient *job*.
C. women feel freer than men to express their feelings, and so respond to criticism more vehemently.
D. they're having their period.

3. You've been telling your best friend's secrets to a sympathetic person. You meant no harm. She finds out and tells you you're an untrustworthy gossip. You

A. get a major migraine.
B. hotly deny you've told any secrets.
C. explain *why* you've divulged her secrets.
D. admit it.

4. You're the junior lawyer in a big firm and expect a promotion to another division of the firm. The senior lawyer in your current division is constantly criticizing your dress, nails, voice—everything except your work, which she has to admit is excellent. Today she tells you that you're far too fat for the corporate image. You

A. feel your eyes well up with tears.
B. promise to go on a diet.
C. smile and nicely say you're sorry she feels that way.
D. resign and look for a job where there are no nasty people employed. Life is too short to accept this kind of aggravation.
E. tell her she has fetid breath.

5. You're the only woman in an advertising firm. You write a report that says the best way to sell the client's product is to take a feminist approach in the advertising. At the weekly conference, your report is ridiculed by a colleague who says, among other things, "Feminism sucks." You

A. tell him *he* sucks.
B. say you have to think about the criticism and will get back to him when you have done that.

C. understand that your report is the victim of sexual politics.

D. tell him that there's no need for vulgarity.

6. You defend your views on Israel at a party. A brilliant woman tells you that you're naive. You
   A. tell her you just happen to have gotten a degree in political science from Yale.
   B. tell her she doesn't know what she's talking about.
   C. disagree firmly, and quietly ask her to be specific.
   D. say to everyone else, "What do you expect from an anti-Semite?"

7. You don't like oral sex. Your lover says he has some constructive criticism for you, which is to see an analyst because you're repressed sexually. You
   A. tell him he's a name-caller and you refuse to play that game.
   B. take his criticism like a sport and make plans to get help.
   C. go down on him.

8. Quote from your mother: "This is not criticism—it's just a suggestion. You look ugly with your hair short." You
   A. ignore her. You can't please everybody.
   B. worry about it a lot, and finally change your hair. After all, your mother really cares about you.
   C. blow your stack at the eighty-year-old.
   D. cut it shorter.

9. Which would you rather have a man give you? Tell the truth!
   A. Dishonest flattery and compliments because he loves you.
   B. Critical judgments because he loves you.
   C. Big bucks, total acceptance, and treatment that makes you feel like a lovable airhead.

10. You teach American literature. Your supervisor comes to observe a class. She then writes a report that says you

don't command the total attention of the class. You think you're a *great* teacher and so, they say, do your students. You're baffled by her report and terribly hurt. You

A. ask her to clarify her statement. What *specifically* caused her to give the negative criticism?

B. ask the kids to sign a petition that clearly states their feelings, and present it to the principal.

C. accept her judgment. After all, she's had more experience than you, but you console yourself with three Big Block Hershey Bars.

D. firebomb her office.

E. flunk the next kid who talks when you're lecturing.

ANSWERS AND ANALYSIS

1. *D* is the answer. You may indeed deserve the criticism. It's too easy to assume jealousy (*B*), self-defense looks silly (*C*), and crippling someone is simply not nice (*A*).

2. *B* is the correct answer. Most men have grown up accepting teammate and coaching criticism and can readily separate this critique of performance from a critique of oneself as a person. Women tend more to think that criticism of a task performed means criticism of self-worth. They often see criticism as an attack on personhood, not on performance.

3. *D* is the only answer here. When you absolutely know adverse criticism is merited, the smoothest way out of the embarrassing situation is simply to own up to it. Convoluted explanations (*C*) are awkward and unbelievable; what's more, excessive apologies make you look weaker and wronger.

4. *C* is the most intelligent choice. Sometimes it's better to grin and bear unfair criticism if that will be the best tactic for your long-term goals. You are simply not going to change her carping, critical nature, and instigating a confrontation might put the kibosh on your promotion. A *B* response indicates a low self-image and a ready victim. An *A* response is just what this bully is looking for. Finally, nasty people are everywhere, Virginia, so *D* is impractical. In an imperfect world, sometimes it's impractical to expect perfect justice.

5. *B* is the answer. It just may be that he understands the client's needs and prejudices better than you do. Perhaps a report written by you as a result of this callous but possibly valid criticism will be met with acceptance. His critique needs checking out.

6. *C* is the only effective response. Asking for specifics doesn't make you look foolish or dumb—it's the *best* way to counter her name-calling. Defending your views by bragging about your education (*A*) or retaliating with name-calling of your own (*B* and *D*) is childish and ineffective.

7. *A* is the answer. Your lover is trying to con you with guilt about something for which you should feel no guilt. Sexual preferences are not to be dictated by others.

8. *A* is the only answer. You *can't* please everyone, and if your mother at eighty is still critical of your hairstyle choice, you will certainly never please her. Consider it an invalid criticism, to be listened to and quietly discarded. If you responded with *D,* you are still in the adolescent-rebellion stage.

9. *B* is the choice of a woman who can deal with criticism without falling apart.

10. *D,* of course, is the ideal choice. No, no, only kidding! Don't firebomb the lady, even if she's dumb enough to deserve it. No, *A* is your answer. She may, when pressed to give specifics, mention the seven kids whispering in the back of the room as you taught. You might explain that you purposely teach in an open-ended atmosphere and *discourage* rigid attention, and that you absolutely disagree with her criticism if that's all it consists of. You might even put your disagreement into a brief note to the administration. It's only fair for you to be allowed to explain your view of things, which may be worlds apart from a very traditional teaching approach. Invalid criticism should be answered, if possible. It may simply stem from a different outlook and approach to a job.

SCORING

Give yourself 10 points for every correct answer.
A score of 90–100 points shows that you can deal with and

learn from valid criticism, and carry on without crumbling with fury, shame, or disgrace from invalid criticism. You do not need constant appreciation and ego massage. All in all, you're a pretty self-assured and together person.

A score of 70-80 indicates a pretty thin skin as far as criticism is concerned. You must learn to include others' negative judgments about you in your life or else be labeled a baby or pompous, arrogant know-it-all. You can do it! Good as you are, you may not be perfect!

A score of 50-60 is rather grim. You take to criticism so poorly that you miss many important lessons. Valid criticism doesn't mean you're a terrible person—it only means you made a mistake or a poor judgment. *Everybody* does that. And invalid criticism is just that—invalid. But it throws you into such a funk, it destroys your confidence—and then, your skill.

A score of under 50 is terrible. Probably you should be criticized even more. You really may *be* a clod (although no doubt a lovable one).

10

Can You Hear What Others Are *Not* Saying?

The gestures people make, the way they sit or hold their heads—the things they *don't* say often give the most revealing and accurate insights into their feelings. Very often, body language can tell you that someone means exactly the opposite of what he's saying. If you're a good people-reader, you are probably popular and successful, because you can not only receive true messages, you send them also. In this quiz circle the answers you think are correct, and then check the analysis to see if you really are adept at hearing the things that people are *not* saying.

1. She sits with legs tightly together, hands clasped in her lap, shoulders hunched forward, chin jutting out. Her message is
   A. "I'm open to suggestions."
   B. "Stay away, hands off."
   C. "I'm shy and frightened."
   D. "I have a terrible urinary infection."

2. As you talk at a cocktail party, he holds his drink straight out in front of him, his arm at a right angle to his body. His message is
   A. "I wish you would go get me another drink, honey. This one is almost finished."

B. "I'm a proper and very uptight person, but I'd like to get to know you better."

C. "I'm keeping you at arm's distance: Don't invade my space."

D. "My arm doesn't bend."

3. You're the boss and you're interviewing someone for a job. He keeps crossing and uncrossing his legs. It probably means that

A. he has trouble making decisions and sticking to them.

B. he is late for another appointment and is uncomfortable about telling you he has to leave.

C. he has to go to the bathroom.

4. He keeps his arms folded on his chest in almost every social situation. It probably means that

A. he doesn't want to hear anyone else's point of view.

B. he feels insecure and defends himself with his arms.

C. he doesn't want anyone to see the perspiration stains under his arms.

5. She seems to caress and stroke her chin an awful lot. This signifies that

A. she is trying to hide a terrible pimple, mole, or wart.

B. she has a chin fetish and is really having a *very* kinky time.

C. she is a cool, thoughtful, and careful person—good in a crisis.

D. she's itching for a fight.

6. You're out with a brilliant new guy, and you like him enormously but have no idea how he feels about you. At dinner he keeps "walking" his fingers on the table toward your plate. Nonverbally, he's saying,

A. "Gimme a french fry."

B. "I have a tricky palsy condition."

C. "Touch me—make contact with me. Let's get to know each other."

D. "I'm bored stiff, and that's why I'm tapping my fingers."

E. "I'd like to feel you up."

7. Your boyfriend always puts his hand on your arm or shoulder when you're at parties, but very rarely touches you that way in private. He
   A. is being affectionate and wants to show the world what a fabulous relationship you have.
   B. is somewhat insecure and touches you to reassure himself of your love.
   C. is involving you in a power display.
   D. is using you for balance.
   E. wants to feel you up.

8. She always starts her sentences with a phrase like, "Truthfully speaking" or "I'll be honest with you." She usually can be counted on to
   A. lie.
   B. be honest and earnest.
   C. say enormously tedious things.

9. He keeps looking at his watch. He
   A. wants to know the time.
   B. is bored out of his gourd.
   C. is a busy man.
   D. is a precise, plan-in-advance person. Also, pretty rude.

10. You're at a cocktail party, don't know anyone, and are deciding which group to join. You choose the group of three who are
    A. sitting on the couch with the two end-people turned in toward the middle person.
    B. sitting on the couch with the two end people crossing their legs away from the middle person.
    C. holding hands and giggling.
    D. having an animated and heated conversation.

11. As the famous author speaks she twists her ring, plays with her bracelet, and runs her hands through her hair. The famous author is
    A. nervous.
    B. annoyed she has to be there.
    C. sizing up the people she's speaking to.

12. You've asked your lover a dozen times to be on time be-
    cause it makes you crazy when he's late. He keeps forget-
    ting how important this is to you. He
    A. really cares for you, and you should be more under-
       standing and less neurotic about punctuality.
    B. is simply a terribly busy person and means nothing
       deeper by his lateness.
    C. is hinting for a new watch. Preferably from Cartier.
    D. must be angry about something.

ANSWERS AND ANALYSIS

1. *B* is what she's telegraphing. It could be *C* except for
the chin jut, which is a sign of defiance, not shyness. Her
closed body posture makes *A* impossible; the fact that she's
hanging around at all makes *D* impossible.

2. *C* is what he's saying. People tend to protect their spa-
tial territory by holding drinks or cigarettes in front of their
bodies, standing behind furniture, etc. This means, "I don't
know you or trust you well enough yet, so stay over there." *B*
is incorrect because nothing about his stance suggests up-
tightness. If you picked *A* or *D*, you're really not so sharp with
body language.

3. *B* is correct; he exhibits a common characteristic of
someone in a hurry to run off. *A* is wrong because leg crossing
has nothing to do with decision-making abilities. As for *C*, if
you know anything about the embarrassing agony of having
to urinate immediately, you know that crossing and uncrossing your legs only aggravates it!

4. Either *A* or *B* is correct, according to most experts on
the language of posture. If you chose *C*, you made the neu-
rotic choice of someone who probably has that problem herself.

5. *C* is the answer! Chin strokers are cautious and cool. *A*
is unlikely. *D* is wrong, because fighters generally stroke their
noses. *B* also is unlikely; one rarely runs into chin fetishists.

6. *C* makes the most sense. *A* is a dopey choice, *B* a flakey one, *D* an insecure one, and *E* is wishful thinking.

7. *C* is the most astute and only correct answer. He's saying, "Lay off, she's mine." If you chose *A* you might wonder why he only touches you like that in public, whereas in private he's rarely affectionate. *B* is wrong for the same reason. *D* is also very wrong unless he has a serious motor problem. If you chose *E* again, *you* have a serious identity problem.

8. *A* is correct: When people are completely honest they have no need to announce their intention of not lying. *B* is not a sensible choice because earnest and honest people just *are:* They don't proclaim it. *C* might be true, but then again her lie might be fascinating.

9. *D* is a good choice—an accurate character sketch of most watch-watchers. *A* is not correct, because one glance would have done it; *B* is wrong because someone *that* bored would have been gone long ago; *C* is wrong because only people who want you to think they're busy would use such an obvious ploy—no truly busy person would.

10. This is a tricky one. *B* is your best choice, because no one on the couch is committed to anyone, and all would probably welcome a new face. The people in *A* are forming a clique by "bookending" the middle person. They are saying, "Hey, we really don't want anyone else here." The people in *C* are rather eccentric, and those in *D* are so involved with each other that a fourth would be an intrusion.

11. Any body language expert would tell you that *A* is the only choice.

12. *D* is correct. Chronic lateness is a well-known sign of hostility. *A* and *B* are self-putdowns. *C* is attributing a little too much subtlety to him.

SCORING

Each correct answer is worth 10 points.

If you scored from 100 to 120 points, you're a superb reader of unspoken language. You can break through the defenses of uptight people because you are able to hear what they cannot say in words. You're sensitive, intelligent, probably a doll!

If you scored from 80 to 90: While you're often correct in your reading of people and situations, you could pay more attention to all the varied and subtle channels of communication in human relations. A little more concentration on the things people do and the things they don't say, and you could be sensational!

If you scored between 60 and 70, you're really not terribly alert to faces, postures, and actions. You're letting the masks of words fool you into thinking they're always truth. Listen with your eyes!

If you scored under 60, you miss most nuances that aren't spelled out in ten-feet-high letters. When it comes to body communication you're on the wrong wavelength! Tune in—you'll start getting nonverbal signals loud and clear.

11

Are You a Good Listener?

If you had to pick one characteristic that successful lovers, friends, and businesspeople share, it would be that they are all acutely sensitive *listeners*. They may not seem as though they're paying attention, but—bet on it—they're catching the most subtle nuances of what you say *and* what you mean. Sometimes you can think you're being a good listener, but then you wonder why you can never remember what the doctor said or find yourself greatly surprised when a friend does an unexpected thing. Take that as a clue that you're not hearing the right messages because you're not listening hard. Take this quiz to see if you're an attentive conversationalist as well as a perceptive one.

1. Your employer invites you into her office and has some highly critical things to say about your performance. During the confrontation, you
   A. concentrate on how she would look naked or on the john.
   B. defend yourself ardently and intelligently.
   C. agree with everything she says. The boss is the boss.
   D. question her statements and ask for further discussion on the points.

2. Having dinner in a restaurant with a friend, you become aware of the conversation of the couple at the next table. It's fascinating. You
   A. half listen to your friend and half focus on the juicy stuff at the next table.
   B. nevertheless tune them out totally, and continue with your own conversation.
   C. tell your friend what has attracted you so you can both listen.

3. At the doctor's office you usually
   A. tune out emotionally because of your nervousness. When you get home, you really haven't a good idea of what has been said.
   B. ask many questions.
   C. listen closely and silently without interrupting.

4. Make a fast mental list of your closest coworker's three main interests. (If you have no coworker, try a friend.)
   A. "OK, I made the list."
   B. "I have no close coworker *or* friend."
   C. "My closest coworker has no big interests."

5. Your lover or husband wants to tell you about his problems. Company's coming in twenty minutes. You
   A. stop what you're doing and listen to him wholeheartedly.
   B. pretend you're all ears and keep making the salad.
   C. give him the tomatoes to cut while you listen.
   D. suggest he save it for his shrink.

6. An office associate asks for your advice with a big problem. She cuts you off when you start to offer it and continues talking about her own decisions. You
   A. feel used. Why did she ask if she doesn't want to hear?
   B. start to doze off.
   C. listen without a word.
   D. force her to face the truth and listen to your ideas.

7. At parties, your general role is
   A. buffoon.

B. center of attraction.

C. to play with conversation the way the Harlem Globe-trotters play with a basketball.

D. windows. You do the windows before the party. Sometimes you do the floors.

8. Do you usually know intimate things about people—secrets?

A. Of course not. I'm a private person and I respect others' privacy.

B. Yes.

C. Only inquisitive people—psychological peeping Toms —crave other peoples' secrets.

9. Your aging mother says she feels achey and sick. She's just had two physical checkups and you know there's nothing wrong. You

A. understand that all older people are a bit hypochondriacal.

B. call the doctor again to show her you really care.

C. spend more time with her.

D. throw her in a nursing home.

10. Your husband says you no longer seem to have much time for him. You'd probably say

A. "We'll discuss it later—I'm busy."

B. "That's the stupidest thing I ever heard. You know I love you."

C. "You're so damned oversensitive."

D. "And what about *me*? Have you noticed how down I feel lately?"

E. "Tell me why you feel that way."

11. When someone tells a long story or joke, invariably you

A. can top it with a better one.

B. love it if it's good, hate it if it's sophomoric.

C. are bored witless.

D. laugh at the wrong places.

12. When your lover, child, or husband tells you about his day, you

A. *look* at him.
B. *feel* your eyes glaze over but act sympathetic.
C. *react* to what you hear with your own impressions.

13. Your man is mainly
    A. your cross to bear.
    B. your confidant.
    C. your consoler.
    D. your most interesting friend.

ANSWERS AND ANALYSIS

1. *D* is the best answer. Imagining her in a ludicrous position is tantamount to shutting out her ideas. And automatically agreeing or disagreeing because she's the boss is not listening either; it's advancing your own position rather than responding to her words.

2. *C* is the best answer. If you said *B* you're probably lying, so what's the good of taking this quiz? It's virtually impossible to ignore a fascinating overheard conversation. A good listener makes a commitment when she's talking with a friend: Either she listens or explains why she can't.

3. *B* is the answer. Asking questions implies you're listening to answers.

4. *A* is the answer that says you're probably a good listener. If you don't listen to people you won't know much about them—that is, if you have anyone left to talk to you.

5. *C* is the best solution for a good listener, because it means sharing the responsibility of preparing for company with your husband—and thus puts you both on equal footing in terms of concentration. One should never pretend to listen. That's patronizing and unfair.

6. *C* is the right answer. Sometimes you have to listen to what's unsaid. It's clear that your associate needs someone to *be* there for her, rather than *give* answers.

7. *C* is a good listener's answer. The Globetrotters pass the ball with great grace because they are constantly aware of

their teammates' positions. They "listen" with their bodies. A good listener at a party will hear what someone else says, respond, and then pass the conversational ball back—not hog it.

8. *B* is the best answer. A person who ends up with others' most secret thoughts is a person who listens and is sympathetic.

9. *C* is right. This is another case of hearing what's not verbally spelled out. People who are lonely or bored often express this with illness. You have to listen hard to the unsaid words to get the message.

10. *E* is the good listener's only possible response. *B* and *C* negate the deep feelings of your husband and attack him by calling him names. *D* turns the problem around so attention is focused on you—a non-listener's ploy. And *A* is proving his point—she *isn't* listening.

11. *B* is listening. The others just pretend to hear.

12. *A* is the answer. A good listener watches body language and facial expressions, which often give a truer message than words.

13. *D* is a good listener's answer. If a lover's most important role is to listen to your secrets, make you feel better when you're sad, or simply irritate you, *you* are not listening to *him*. Maybe he's boring or maybe you're selfish. In either case, either reconsider your lover or improve your listening habits.

SCORING

Give yourself 10 points for every correct answer.

A score of 120–130 points proves you're superattentive and really there for your friends. You know how to give conversational feedback when it's called for, and when to be just a steady, listening, silent presence. You're alert to the world, and probably pretty popular.

A score of 90–110 indicates some listening lapses, although it's not bad at all. Understand that no one can be responsive to conversation 100 percent of the time. Instead of faking interest you ought to explain distractions. Weigh what people say: Try to hear the meanings instead of just the words. Look at speakers. You're usually a wonderful conversational partner, but could use some self-reminders to concentrate.

A score of 60–80 indicates a tone-deaf, meaning-deaf listener. You're too self-involved to really hear others. Relax. Try to pay attention to others' needs. In listening better you'll not only find people more interesting, they'll respect and appreciate you more.

A score of below 60? Maybe it's ear wax.

12

What's Your Love Style?

Variety is what puts the punch into life, and if your sugar daddy likes little girls in pinafores and you like to wear pinafores—terrific! On the other hand, if it seems that you're attracting every sponger and crazy and jealous weirdo in the book, and you hate it, it could be because you're hooked on some kind of self-destructive love style. Often our insecurities cause us to choose, in subtle and insidious ways, those people who are most wrong for us. And don't blame it on bad luck. We create our own love cycles, and can revolve in any path from a vicious circle to a healthy, heavenly orbit. If you're suffering more than you're giggling, giving more than you're getting—your love style may need a drastic reappraisal.

This is a quiz with no scoring because its point is not to indicate right answers but to identify your love-style pattern. If something sounds flakey to others but makes you happy, go in peace. If it's destructive, and you're unhappy with the lovers you choose, perhaps your own shaky needs are dictating unsatisfying relationships. Decide, and remember—you can always change your love style if you really want to.

1. Which of the following women *best* (if not completely) reflects your love style?

A. Linda Lovelace
B. Pia Zadora
C. Liv Ullmann
D. Jane Fonda
E. Mary Worth
F. Joan of Arc

2. The men who are most attractive to you
    A. are the ones who are dependable, above all.
    B. are usually touched by sadness and tragedy, and spend a lot of time brooding darkly and staring into space.
    C. are usually sweet and quite funny.
    D. are those who keep you guessing.
    E. have massive sexual organs.

3. You'd like best to sleep with your lover
    A. in your own bed on plain white sheets.
    B. in the motel bed in which you made glorious love last night, in between the same sweaty and wrinkled sheets.
    C. in a canopied bed under the stars.
    D. in a crib.

4. Which of the following turns you on sexually or romantically? (Check as many as you wish.)
    A. playing dirty-word scrabble
    B. reading about or watching a lesbian scene
    C. having an intense argument and then making up
    D. having deep eye contact with a stranger at a party
    E. direct praise of your breasts, hips, or behind
    F. a bubble bath, an oiled body, a glass of wine
    G. being pinched, scratched, or gouged
    H. Daddy coming for dinner
    I. when your man is visibly attracted to another woman
    J. when he is abusive to you because he's quite jealous
    K. broccoli

5. Which one belongs to you?
    A. Your lover always tells you how terrific you look until you get to where you're going. *Then* he helpfully

points out that your pants seem too tight or your dress is out of place and your makeup's too heavy. Also, when he breaks dates (often) he uses such bad excuses it almost seems as if he wants you to know he's lying.

B. Your lover is the cuddliest, cutest thing. He lets you shop for him, make him stuffed derma, and tend to his hemmorhoids and appointment book. He's great in bed and makes a woman feel *needed*.

C. Your lover is a strong, dynamite, take-charge guy. Even though beige makes you look like Wheatena, you wear it because it's his favorite color. No wishy-washy he: The play you'll see, the restaurant at which you'll dine, and the best business moves for you are usually decided by him in advance.

D. Your lover is a big-bicepsey brute. He's a kisser and a hugger but seems to choose anything in preference to actual sexual intercourse. Also, when you do manage to get him to bed, he can't seem to achieve orgasm unless he's wearing a fuzzy thing. This puzzles you.

6. Your last bed partner might well describe you as
   A. all starry eyes and candlelight and poetry.
   B. a good sport who puts up with what he likes, even though you're not crazy about dressing up as a shepherdess.
   C. enigmatic. He never knows whether you hate it or love it or whether he should ever do it again.
   D. lusty and adventuresome and loving.
   E. comatose.

7. You're intrigued by him. Now he has suggested a trial living-together session. He seems terrific, but you know he has dropped four women in the last year. You say
   A. no. He has a poor track record and you are afraid of being another head in his collection.
   B. yes. You're special and individual and what he and you have together has nothing to do with anyone else in his past.
   C. yes—*if* he promises to be absolutely faithful and com-

mitted to the relationship. This means no lunches, telephone conversations, gifts exchanged with any other woman.

8. The best present he could bring you tonight would be
   A. news that he got a promotion and he's not coming home because he has to celebrate with his coworkers.
   B. black lace underwear.
   C. a book of Shakespearean love sonnets.
   D. a new broiler oven.
   E. wild flowers he picked himself.
   F. an expensive blouse his mother picked out for you. (She has great taste.)

9. With which sentence do you most agree? A love relationship is
   A. a preordained process. Whatever happens will happen, and one must make the best of what one has.
   B. an upward struggle in which one ultimately stands alone. One must be careful and defensive in order to survive.
   C. a process that calls for great contributions on each side if both are to reap great rewards.
   D. a frail thing with as much chance of surviving as Ali McGraw had in *Love Story*.
   E. a complex game.

10. Which of the couples below seem to have a relationship and love style worth emulating?
    A. Pat and Dick Nixon
    B. Elizabeth Barrett and Robert Browning
    C. Marquis de Sade and any friend
    D. Prince Charles and Lady Di
    E. Svengali and Trilby
    F. Gertrude Stein and Alice B. Toklas

ANSWERS AND ANALYSIS

1. An *A* choice implies your willingness to be a sex *object* in your love style. A *B* choice suggests a baby doll looking for

a daddy image. A *C* choice points to a romantic love style. *D* suggests an independent and creative one. *E* says you're happiest being someone's Mommy. And *F* points to a self-martyring love style—a losing one.

2. If you chose *A*, you no doubt prize safety so much you'd give up challenge and excitement. If *B* is your man, you enjoy being tortured by an egocentric victim. A *C* choice says you no doubt have a good self-image and an ability to choose a mate who matches. On the other hand, choosing *D* men implies that you get a sick kick out of being manipulated. If it's *E* you circled, didn't anyone ever tell you the difference between quality and quantity? Those that are massive may be quite passive.

3. If you chose *A* your love style shows a delight in being safe. You're passionate but slobbish if you circled *B*. A *C* choice suggests an impractical, sometimes childish, romantic. A *D* choice suggests you're in big trouble.

4. You have a masochistic love style if you show a pattern of being turned on by either physical hurt (*G*) or emotional hurt (*I* and *J*). *C* is not a terrific choice either because it shows you lean toward game-playing relationships in which anger is often used. It can backfire! If Daddy (*H*) turns you on, your shrink *and* your mother ought to be notified. If broccoli (*K*) does it for you—well, at least it's better than asparagus which turns your pee green. *B* is a fairly common turn-on for many women. If it's the *only* thing that turns you on perhaps you're harboring a latent tendency toward homosexuality in your love style. Remember, nothing is wrong with whatever turns you on unless it involves pain to someone else—which is why any of the other choices are quite reasonable.

5. You're not to be envied if *any* of these galoots belong to you. *A* is a sadistic, malicious wretch, and what's wrong with *you* for putting up with him? *B* makes you feel needed because he is abnormally needy. You have a pretty low self-image if you are caught up in this one-way love style. *C* is a domineering, critical male chauvinist. If you allow yourself to be molded into his idea of what's good, you're awfully weak. *D* may be yearning for a platonic relationship because of a latent homosexuality. The fuzzy thing is extremely creepy.

6. If you chose *A*, you're a pure romantic in terms of love style. If you chose *B*, you are a bit of a martyr and probably cheat yourself a lot. If you chose *C*, you're involved in a game-playing relationship. *E* implies a very dead relationship. A *D* answer is, of course, the sign of a healthy, zestful love style.

7. *A* means you're a smart cookie. *B* means you're a self-punishing, "natural-victim" cookie. And *C* means you think you'd thrive in a possessive and childish relationship—a self-deceiving cookie.

8. *A* indicates that you are a martyr in your love style and no one ever loves a martyr. *B* is a nice, sexually titillating choice, and *C* a nice romantically and intellectually titillating choice. If you chose *D*, you have a most pedestrian and dull love style, unless of course you have some kinky things you two do with that broiler oven. *E* is delicious as a love offering. If you chose *F*, you encourage a great dependence on his mother. *No* expensive blouse is worth that kind of interference in a relationship.

9. *A* shows a resigned and probably not very imaginative love style. *B* shows a very nervous love style. It *can't* feel great. *C* shows a partnership approach to love which is always gratifying. *D* shows a pretty negative attitude toward love. *E* indicates a manipulative and game-playing personality—bound to be destructive.

10. If ever there was a "follow my leader" relationship, it's *A*. Did she *ever* look fulfilled with him? *B* is a romantic and brave and colorful couple. If you think *C* is appealing, you probably like nails under the mattress and enemas as well. *D* is hardly an *equal* relationship for a liberated woman. *E* is a horror-movie couple. *F* is also a case of leader and follower.

13

How Well Do You Communicate Your Sexual Desires?

Because you're such a *nice* person as well as a wonderfully wise and witty one, any minute now Mr. Wonderful will come from the wings to pleasure you and give you the sexual confidence you need, not to mention orgasms. Right? Not right. Even though you *deserve* him, and even if he has made an appearance already, you, like every woman, are responsible for your own sexual pleasure. There's no lying back and waiting for the earth to move. In a way, selfishness is called for during sexual relations, because without concentrating on your needs (as much as, if not more than, your partner) you cannot achieve total satisfaction. Naturally, a warm, attentive partner will work toward satisfying your needs as well as his own. But if you don't let him know what you think is swell, if you don't let him know what you think, period—then don't get angry when your lovemaking is less than powerful. Some women find it difficult to communicate their sexual needs freely because they get embarrassed or their partners become hostile or hurt when they do so. If that's your problem, it's a serious one. Do something about changing your habits of communication, or else be satisfied thinking about laundry lists in the thick of the action.

Circle one response to each of the following questions to see how effectively you're able to talk about your sexual needs.

Then check out the analysis at the end to see what your answers tell you about you.

1. When you feel like making love, you let your partner know by
   A. drawing arrows on your body in lipstick pointing to your breasts and vagina.
   B. leaving a note on the mirror.
   C. giving him a secret hand signal and hoping he loves you enough to understand it.
   D. gently stroking his face or thigh.
   E. cutting out *Playgirl* and *Playboy* centerfolds, stapling them together in compromising positions, and leaving them lying casually around the den.

2. In order to tell someone what turns you on, you have to be familiar with your own body. Which of these statements are most nearly true for you?
   A. "I think my clitoris is somewhere near my belly button."
   B. "I think there are some really disgusting smells that come from me."
   C. "I have run my hands over and into my body and I am amazed at its complexity and sweetness."
   D. "I really don't like to look at myself naked in the mirror."
   E. "During intercourse I try to remember to hold my stomach in."

3. If you told your partner graphically just what you would like him to do to you during lovemaking, you think he would
   A. guffaw.
   B. vomit.
   C. think you were crude.
   D. tell his shrink.
   E. do it.

4. If your partner does something to you that hurts during your lovemaking, would you most likely

A. pant loudly and pretend you love it?

B. say "Ouch"?

C. say nothing?

D. knee or pinch him hard?

E. muffle your scream?

5. How often do you initiate lovemaking?
   A. About as often as he does.
   B. Never. You don't want him to think you're a nympho-maniac, after all.
   C. Six or more times a day.

6. If your sexual partner does something you really like, you would probably
   A. sing the Hallelujah Chorus.
   B. tell him to do it again.
   C. be extraordinarily careful he doesn't find out how good it felt, because that would embarrass you terribly.
   D. let him know by the way you move your body how terrific it was.
   E. buy him an expensive gift.

7. Your lover is delightful in all respects but one. His breath is absolutely fetid and it colors your sexual moments a darkish green. What would you do about it?
   A. Write him an anonymous letter.
   B. Say "Arrgh" or "Yecch" whenever he tries to kiss you.
   C. Swallow your disgust and concentrate on his fine qualities.
   D. Tell him gently, but tell him yourself.
   E. Ask him to blow into a small balloon. Then let the air escape back into his face, and say, "Guess what?"

8. When you experience orgasm you
   A. try to keep it a secret so he won't think you're so impressed with him.
   B. don't hesitate to scream, moan, or giggle—whatever comes naturally.
   C. yawn.
   D. claw his back and beat on his head.

9. What does your partner think you think?
   A. "Sex is necessary but not something that takes first priority in my life."
   B. "There is nowhere I'd rather be than in bed with him."
   C. "There is nothing more repellent than thick, white, mucousy semen."
   D. "Life is a fountain."

10. "There are certain things my lover likes to do that really turn me off during our lovemaking.
    A. But I'd never hurt his feelings by telling him *which* things."
    B. I must really be frigid because everyone else likes to do those things. Anyway it would embarrass me to mention it."
    C. I couldn't possibly tell him, though, because he'd get so angry and irritated."
    D. It's my responsibility to tell my partner even though he's clearly enjoying them."
    E. It's kind of difficult for me to say anything with the gag in my mouth. If it weren't for the handcuffs, I suppose I could use sign language."

ANSWERS AND ANALYSIS

1. *D,* of course, is the correct answer. If you chose *A,* you need a course in "How to Be Subtle." *B* is an avoidance technique. *C* shows a Nancy Drew mentality. *E* is somewhat too dramatic.

2. *C* is the answer that is lovely. If you chose *A*—well, perhaps your belly button is more creative than mine. *B* indicates either that you have a serious problem or you haven't bathed in a while. As for *D*—well, *work on* looking at and liking yourself better. If you chose *E,* why not just wear a girdle during intercourse?

3. *E* is the partner we'd all like. Throw *A* out on his stupid ear; *B* needs some Maalox and a few months of intensive therapy. *C* probably can't get it up, and as for *D*—well, I guess he's trying but it's his problem, not yours.

4. Only *B* is not masochistic or overreacting. Choice *A* indicates a bit of a fool. *C* is a martyr who shouldn't really expect pleasure if she's unable to be honest about pain. *D* seems to be an overreaction. *E* either has watched too many late movies or has an unseemly amount of difficulty in communication.

5. If you chose *A,* good for you! *B* is operating in 1942. *C* is either *very* taken with her lover or has nothing else to do.

6. If you chose *D,* you're a communicative and responsive person. If you chose *B,* you're a little blunter, but absolutely correct also. If you chose *A,* you have a problem, because your response may just break the romantic mood. A *C* response should tell you that you have some significant sexual hangups. An *E* response is overdoing your gratitude a little. Try doing something *he* likes a lot, instead of getting the fourteen-karat gold tie clasp.

7. A *D* choice illustrates your bravery and honesty. You probably have great success sexually. If you chose *A,* you're a dirty coward, but I have to admit I'd choose it, too. If you went for *B,* don't be amazed if he doesn't call you again or if he cries. A *C* answer indicates that you're playing martyr again. Face it: You won't be able to think of one fine quality with green breath all over you. Now if you chose *E,* Johnny Carson might be interested in your cute trick, but your lover would think you addleheaded.

8. *B* indicates a natural and responsive communicator. *A* indicates a games-player and a loser. *C* indicates intense boredom—and a poor orgasm. *D* indicates an understandably unpopular form of sexual communication.

9. *B* means your partner is fortunate to be picking up such vibes. *A* indicates your partner is getting the impression that your boardroom is far superior to his bedroom, and that's not a terrific impression to give. As for *C*—if you chose this one, rest assured, Madam, your partner will never again achieve an erect state in your presence. And if you chose *D,* you're both a little flakey.

10. *D* is the only correct answer. As I said above, your own pleasure is your own job. If you chose *A,* you are never destined for bigger things in bed. What's more, he probably

would not be hurt at all, but would appreciate your candor. A *B* answer is a very wrong answer. Blaming things on frigidity shows you lack the interest and courage to work things out through communication. If your answer was *C*, tough gazoobies on your partner! As for *E*—are you *sure* those things really turn you off?

SCORING

Give yourself 2 points for every answer that shows you to be a super sexual communicator.

If your score is between 18 and 20 points, your love life should be terrific, because you are mature and intelligent in your ability to touch—really touch—your partner with your deepest sensitivities. If, despite this, your love life is not terrific, you are hanging out with the wrong guy. He doesn't understand about grown-up sexuality.

If your score is between 14 and 16, you need to learn to expose your vulnerabilities a little more. You probably know that it's your responsibility to achieve your own sexual satisfaction, but you're hung up on games-playing and your worry that honesty will turn him off. Courage! You're special, and telling him of your special needs can only turn him on.

If your score is between 10 and 12, you really need some artificial respiration because your whole body must be deadened to pleasure. Worrying about just *his* needs cheats you cruelly. Be assertive! Speak up!

If you scored under 10, you're missing the whole point of this book. Join an encounter group. Or get thee to a nunnery.

14

How Much Do You Really Know About Your Man?

Intimate and lasting relationships are based upon real mutual understanding. Very often we live with someone and have never touched his true core—the deepest, most sensitive part of him—because we haven't delved deeply enough into his past or his innermost feelings. To know someone, *really* know him, you ought to be able to anticipate his probable reactions and opinions as well as be familiar with his past and present. This, then, is a quiz for two: Take it and answer these questions about your man; then let him take it. Compare your answers to see how well you really know him.

His Past

1. In high school, he dated
   A. Ms. Class Intellectual.
   B. Miss Pom-Pom Girl.
   C. Miss Betsy Tight-Sweater.
   D. no one. He was too short.
   E. the ugliest girl. He always was kind to unfortunates.
   F. Stanley Marcus.

2. If he ever ran away from home, where did he run?
   A. to his house of worship

    B. to a relative's house
    C. to a friend's house
    D. to the circus

3. If he knew Walter Venters was waiting outside of school to beat him up, he would have
    A. shit in his pants.
    B. told the teacher.
    C. gone outside to fight with Walter.
    D. tried to reason Walter out of it, using cool logic.

4. A likely hero for your man in his youth could have been
    A. Mussolini.
    B. Jackie Robinson.
    C. Nelson Rockefeller.
    D. e.e. cummings.
    E. Walter Venters.

5. The fondest dream of his youth was to
    A. become rich.
    B. become famous.
    C. have a deeply satisfying romantic and sexual attachment.
    D. get on the team.
    E. kill Walter Venters.

6. His relationship with his parents was
    A. devoted.
    B. cordial.
    C. destructive.
    D. strained.
    E. kinky.

His Present

7. If his daughter told him she was pregnant and wanted to have an abortion, he would likely say,
    A. "I'll kill the guy."
    B. "Let's talk about it."
    C. "God punished you for your filth."

D. "The ERA people did this."

E. "Do whatever you want."

8. Tops on his list of *Worst Things That Could Happen* is that

    A. he'll lose his sexual potency.

    B. he'll lose the account.

    C. he'll lose you.

    D. he'll lose his mommy's love.

    E. he'll lose his control.

    F. he'll lose a good friend.

    G. Walter Venters will find him.

9. In his heart of hearts, he yearns for people to

    A. think of him with respect.

    B. think of him with love.

    C. think that he's very strong and masculine and sexy.

    D. think that he's very intelligent.

    E. give him money.

10. Which comes closest to his real belief?

    A. The women's liberation movement is also liberating to men.

    B. The women's liberation movement has gone too far.

    C. The women's liberation movement is run by a group of misguided lesbians.

    D. "I wish the women's liberation movement hadn't come into my life. I know it's important but I wish *my* woman would stay home."

    E. "The Communists started the whole thing."

His Future

11. When he's sixty-five and of retirement age, he will probably be concerned with

    A. selling the house and moving to Florida.

    B. continuing what he's doing today.

    C. fourteen-year-olds' pudenda.

    D. *your* pudendum.

E. boats.

F. death.

12. To him, the future looks
    A. bleak.
    B. frightening.
    C. challenging.
    D. peaceful.
    E. crappy.

General

13. Almost every day he feels
    A. misunderstood.
    B. taken advantage of.
    C. unappreciated.
    D. successful.
    E. himself up.

14. When something wounds him emotionally, he
    A. clams up and wants to be left alone.
    B. would really like to share the pain but finds it difficult to talk.
    C. blames the whole thing on you.
    D. needs you.

15. The thing he likes best about you is your
    A. sense of humor.
    B. warmth.
    C. inventiveness.
    D. big knockers.
    E. parents' stocks.

SCORING

Give yourself 10 points every time he agrees with your choice of answers.

If you scored 130–150 points, you can feel confident that you are your man's best friend as well as lover. There's no doubt that you're tuned in to his psyche and his *essence*. You've taken the time to find out who he really is and what he cares about. He's a lucky man, and you probably have a supportive and cheerful relationship.

If you scored 100-120, you're surely in touch with his thinking, but perhaps you would both benefit from some really deep, soul-searching talks. Hear him out but remember, he may speak more eloquently when he's silent than when he talks. You have to learn to listen to the silences as well as the words. Clearly, you're missing *some* of the clues he radiates. A little more thinking about his needs might make the difference between a good rapport and an extraordinary one.

If you scored 80-90, you really are both missing out on communication. If you missed six or seven responses out of the fifteen, that's too many. Ask him some pointed questions about his needs, his beliefs, his fears—sit down and talk! If you know so little about him, he probably knows less about you. You must take the love you obviously share and enhance it with deeper understanding. You can start with talking about some of the questions on this quiz: Find out more about *why* he answered the way he did.

If you scored under 80, you're living with a virtual stranger. If you think you're happy, you must have some terrific sex life that makes up for all other communication. Either that, or you just met.

15

How Well Do You Fit into His Support System?

You're serious about him and considering a committed relationship or even marriage. His support system is vital to his life style—which you're going to be sharing—and you'd better be compatible with the key people in his life. Are you?

1. The first thing that pops into your mind when you think of his brother is,
   A. "Schmuck!"
   B. "I wonder if he makes more than Jeff."
   C. "If he tells one more joke, I'll scream."
   D. "Do I have a nice girl for you!"
   E. "Mmm—that telltale bulge is darling."

2. He sees his shrink weekly. You feel
   A. jealous that he's telling his secrets to someone else.
   B. annoyed at the big bucks he's shelling out.
   C. relieved that his violent tendencies may soon be cured.
   D. happy that he seeks direction or help if he needs it.
   E. slightly repelled at this "weakness," even though you hate to admit it.

3. He says his business requires a certain amount of time to be spent in nighttime socialization with his professional peers, and that does not include you. You think

    A. he's playing around.

    B. it's either them or you.

    C. you'd better find yourself something fun and interesting to do.

    D. he overdoes it.

4. His best friend calls you a "bad feminist" to your face. You

    A. punch him out (his best friend, that is).

    B. demand an apology.

    C. call him a macho pig.

    D. ask him what's a bad feminist?

5. His children are

    A. your sworn enemies.

    B. a pain in the ass.

    C. taking too much of his time.

    D. OK.

    E. malevolent.

6. His dog

    A. makes on the rug.

    B. will have to go.

    C. reminds you of your childhood stuffed toy.

    D. terrifies you.

7. He's got a really high fever and feels lousy. His mother comes rushing over with chicken soup and aspirin. You

    A. step back.

    B. think she's smothering him.

    C. make him his favorite pâté and shrimp curry.

    D. leave.

8. After a particularly exhausting day, he loves to stop off at the neighborhood bar to have a beer and a chat with his favorite bartender. You

    A. secretly think he should come home for the beer.

    B. think this is *very* low class.

    C. think the bartender sounds charming and you suggest meeting him there one day.

9. He's been going to Guido's for haircuts for seven years and his hair is cut unfashionably short. He *likes* Guido's.

You wish he'd try François, your last boyfriend's barber, because he does such a fabulous job. You

A. tell him you've seen roaches at Guido's.

B. learn to love his haircuts.

C. won't sleep with him on haircut days.

D. hate his haircuts but can live with them.

10. His uncle (or boss or friend or brother) has made an obnoxious sexual overture to you. You

A. have a serious anxiety attack.

B. never tell him. You can handle it, and why should you crush his faith in that person?

C. tell him as fast as you can get the words out.

11. His boss admires Polish jokes, subservient women, and segregated schools. He thinks Ronald Reagan is a great wit. He invites you and your boyfriend to his home for some "good talk." You

A. can't possibly go.

B. go and defend your beliefs.

C. go and zipper your lip.

12. Your man has an old girlfriend whom he has definitely "outgrown," he says, but whom he still respects for her business acumen. You can understand that, but you are definitely uncomfortable when she hangs out at your home. You

A. decide your feelings are childish and nonsupportive and resolve to grow up.

B. absolutely refuse to have her as a guest in your home.

C. spill things on her when she comes over, acting adorable all the while so he can get his priorities straight.

D. stay away for those evenings when he wants her to come over.

ANSWERS AND ANALYSIS

1. *D* is the only response that indicates a healthy attitude toward his brother. If you're jealous of, bored with, or attracted to his beloved sibling, there's bound to be trouble.

2. Again, *D* is the reasonable response. *A* is childish and unsophisticated. *B* is terribly selfish and an indication that you'd make his life miserable. *E* shows total incompatibility. As for *C,* if he has violent tendencies you'd better get going while the going's good.

3. *C* is the response of an adult who respects her peer's professional life. Everything else portends many moments of tension.

4. What *is* a bad feminist? That's the question for discussion, isn't it? Other answers simply indicate a lack of self-confidence on your part. *D* is the choice.

5. If the answer's not *D,* you've got a real problem, for it's unlikely that he's going to renounce his children for you. *C* is perhaps negotiable. (If you chose *C,* give yourself 5 points.)

6. Animals are very definitely part of the support system of an animal lover. If you hate or are terrified by Bonzo, it's not going to be easy. *C,* then, is the response with the most positive possibilities. *A* can be dealt with at dog-training school (5 points for *A*).

7. Step back, girl, step back (*A*). If you can't and end up vying with his mother, you're a fool. Unless she's really Mrs. Portnoy, cope with her. If you chose *C,* your man is going to vomit.

8. *C* is the adult response. You are not on the same wavelength at all if you can't see the palliative effect his neighborhood bartender has on him.

9. *D* is the answer. You can't make him neat and you can't change his barber. Everyone knows that.

10. *C* is the answer. His support system takes second place to your sexual integrity. He should certainly know, anyway, that his support system isn't so supportive.

11. The answer is *A*. It's dumb to get into a hassle with his boss, and you can't possibly go and allow everything you believe in to be attacked. In this case, being compatible with his support system means staying far away. It can be done.

12. Your answer is *B*. This is a crucial and dangerous question. Any man who would inflict an old girlfriend on you when you hate it is definitely acting out hostile tendencies. What's more, you shouldn't have to be uncomfortable in your own

home or avoid that home. No one's going to think you're aw-fully adorable with the spilling act. If he *must* see her, let it be on his time—and you'll have to decide whether his business interests are legitimate or hostile.

SCORING

Give yourself 10 points for every correct answer (except where 5 is specified).

A score of 100-120 points indicates that you respect and understand his support system and should shortly be an integral part of it. Even if you don't love everybody he loves, you have the warmth, wisdom, and ability to accept them. If he's as responsive to the people *you* need, your relationship looks blessed.

A score of 80-90 should tell you that although you probably have similar instincts about people, there are going to have to be some accommodations made on your part. Much heart-to-heart communication between you is necessary to determine just to what extent he needs you to embrace his cohorts and how much you're willing to give. You might have to mute the jagged edges of your response to his people.

A score of 60-70 is a pretty poor showing and predicts trouble for the two of you. You simply don't revolve in the orbit of those who buoy and delight him. Are you competing with him or plotting against him—or planning to be his best friend? If it's not the latter, you'd better rethink your commitment.

If you scored below 60, he needs you about as much as he needs a third nostril. Ditto for your need for him.

16

Have You Had It with Harry?

Harry, if you care to admit it, has been a pain. Sure, he still has all these interesting qualities that first drew you to him, but lately he's been argumentative, sullen, and—yes, say it—*boring*. Just a little boring, anyway. You've been wondering if it isn't time to sever the relationship—and wondering if he isn't wondering the same thing. Then again, perhaps this is just a temporary rocky phase, and if you stick it out you'll have something more solid than ever.

This quiz is designed to measure the reality and quality of your togetherness. Check each answer that comes closest to the truth. No lying allowed. Points off for lying, as a matter of fact.

Sexuality

1. You'd rather
   A. read Plato alone than the Kama Sutra with Harry.
   B. fake an orgasm than explain to Harry why it wasn't terrific.
   C. make love with Harry than go to an orgy with Robert Redford and Burt Reynolds.
   D. eat Fig Newtons.

2. If sex is a banquet, you'd compare your love life with Harry to
   A. a smorgasbord.
   B. a bad Chinese meal (in an hour you're hungry again).
   C. a lettuce-and-tomato sandwich.
   D. chopped Hamburger Helper with lots of ketchup.

3. When you think of making love with Harry, you're reminded of
   A. the earth moving.
   B. trying abstinence as a sexual option.
   C. crackers in bed.
   D. Gypsies.

4. Not that you're into bestiality, but Harry in bed is most like
   A. a circus bear.
   B. a hamster.
   C. a fox.
   D. a stallion.

5. He considers your sexual satisfaction
   A. almost always.
   B. never.
   C. sometimes.
   D. once a month.

6. A satisfying sexual experience is most often started by
   A. a rousing argument.
   B. an X-rated flick.
   C. a good laugh with some horseplay thrown in.
   D. his dressing up in your best high heels and Dior panty hose.

Friendship and Togetherness

7. Your life together in terms of books is best described as
   A. *War and Peace*
   B. *The Final Days*

C. *Between Parent and Child*
D. *Paradise Regained*
E. *Mein Kampf*

8. A week without Harry would be
   A. heaven.
   B. lonely.
   C. interesting.
   D. tension free.

9. Harry and you generally deal with arguments by
   A. being cleverly sarcastic.
   B. Harry winning.
   C. hitting, pinching, a little spitting.
   D. talking it out.
   E. walking away from each other and not talking for a while.

10. If you call him at work, he
    A. is embarrassed and annoyed.
    B. is delighted!
    C. wants to get to the point of the call immediately.
    D. puts you on hold.

11. If he calls you at work, you
    A. wish everybody could hear how cute he is.
    B. can't wait to get back to what you were doing.
    C. hang up.
    D. think he must be neglecting some important work of his own.

12. Your relationship can best be described as a trip to
    A. the steam bath.
    B. the Istanbul bazaar.
    C. your mother's house.
    D. the corner.

You, Harry, and the Rest of the World

13. His relationship to your family and friends keeps you
    A. explaining away his moods.

    B. wanting to hug him.

    C. tense.

    D. nauseous.

14. At parties, Harry tends to

    A. disappear until it's time to go home.

    B. become jealous and anxious whenever you're involved in conversations that don't include him.

    C. put lampshades on his head.

    D. circulate easily by himself but check in with you periodically for a kiss or squeeze.

15. He thinks of the rest of the world as

    A. a Rubik's Cube.

    B. tedious.

    C. a playpen.

    D. an enemy.

16. He compares you with other women

    A. all the time, and it's a damned drag.

    B. never.

    C. never, except for his mother.

    D. never, verbally, but you see him looking and touching too often.

17. Sometimes

    A. the way he laughs embarrasses you.

    B. the way he dresses embarrasses you.

    C. the way he looks when he doesn't know you're watching him makes you melt.

    D. he's a nerd.

Singing the Blues

18. When he's unhappy

    A. you worry about him, but don't dare approach him because there will be some sort of an explosion.

    B. he gets maudlin and cries a lot.

    C. you can't wait to get to his side and hold him.

    D. you're secretly glad.

19. When you're unhappy he
    A. says he knows it's his fault and keeps apologizing for his face, his ways, his heritage, his etc.
    B. has a drink.
    C. tells you to pull yourself together.
    D. encourages you to talk until you get to the root of the problem.

Commitment

20. Whenever you question your commitment to Harry, you think that
    A. you'd break up with Harry if you weren't so afraid of being alone.
    B. Harry's gotten weird.
    C. there's a whole world of interesting people out there who'd appreciate you more than Harry does.
    D. no matter what, you always want to wake up with Harry on your pillow.

21. Recently, it's been too much trouble to
    A. stay faithful to Harry.
    B. discuss your business and life plans with him.
    C. wash your face before you go to bed with Harry.
    D. answer the phone when you know he's calling.
    E. be nice to the attractive guy in the office.

Your View of the Future

22. Spending the rest of your life with Harry would be comparable to
    A. a subway ride.
    B. a luxury cruise.
    C. a bicycle built for two.
    D. jogging uphill.

23. If Harry were to have an affair with someone else next year, you'd be
    A. sick about it.

B. not terribly surprised.
C. relieved.
D. furious.

24. One day, Harry will be
    A. a cold but respected business success.
    B. a sweet, funny, delicious guy, just the way he is now.
    C. a dirty old man.
    D. ugly.
    E. in jail.

25. When Harry makes a promise to you, you know he
    A. prays he can make it good one day.
    B. is lying through his teeth.
    C. wants something from you.
    D. will work as hard as possible to make it happen.

And finally,
26. Harry is
    A. indispensable.
    B. cute when he's mad.
    C. irritating.
    D. a 189-pound weight on your heart.
    E. sincere.

SCORING

OK, now give yourself points as follows:

1.	A:2	B:0	C:3	D:−1	
2.	A:3	B:1	C:1	D:1	
3.	A:3	B:−1	C:1	D:2	
4.	A:1	B:−1	C:2	D:3	
5.	A:3	B:−1	C:1	D:0	
6.	A:0	B:2	C:3	D:−1	
7.	A:1	B:1	C:0	D:3	E:−3
8.	A:−2	B:3	C:0	D:1	
9.	A:1	B:0	C:−3	D:3	E:1

10.	A:−1	B:3	C:1	D:0	
11.	A:3	B:−1	C:−1	D:1	
12.	A:0	B:3	C:2	D:1	
13.	A:1	B:3	C:0	D:−2	
14.	A:2	B:0	C:0	D:3	
15.	A:3	B:1	C:2	D:−1	
16.	A:−3	B:3	C:0	D:1	
17.	A:1	B:1	C:3	D:−1	
18.	A:2	B:1	C:3	D:−1	
19.	A:1	B:0	C:0	D:3	
20.	A:1	B:−1	C:1	D:3	
21.	A:1	B:1	C:1	D:−1	E:3
22.	A:0	B:3	C:2	D:−1	
23.	A:3	B:1	C:0	D:2	
24.	A:1	B:3	C:−1	D:0	E:−3
25.	A:2	B:−1	C:−1	D:3	
26.	A:3	B:2	C:−1	D:−3	E:2

Add up the total amount of points, making sure you subtract when necessary. If you have lied, even a little, take off another 5 points!

If you have scored over 69 points, Harry is a prince. Don't, for God's sake, dump him. Perhaps you've had one or two fallings-out that have left you feeling angry or hurt, but they're no doubt aberrations that don't reflect the true essence of your relationship. If you can't make it with Harry, you are going to have real trouble making it with anyone. A real doll, that Harry.

If you've scored between 56 and 68 points, don't be hasty. Think about the time he brought you the hot-fudge sundae when you had that facially deforming cold, think about how swell his bottom looks, think about how your heart stopped when he caught his finger in the car door. Harry is definitely a sweet guy, but perhaps both of you could use some lessons in communication. Listen, he's not exactly a prince, but maybe by this time Lady Di doesn't think Charles is such a prince either.

If you've scored under 56 points, OUT, OUT with Harry! You have had it with him. He's a life-destroying force: *your* life. Get rid of his teeth retainer and his special cup, also—the one that says Big Daddy.

YOU
and How You Work with Others

17

Can You Ace an Interview?

The interview: There isn't a job-hunting course or manual that ignores its crucial importance. Often, the person who gets the job is not necessarily the most qualified applicant but the one who sells herself best. If you can convince the interviewer that you're the perfect, most exciting choice for the job, your credentials take second place. There are certain basics in interviewing, the most obvious being dressing appropriately (plaid polyester suits or dangling earrings are *not* appropriate unless you're interviewing for High Tack Magazine), arriving on time, writing a follow-up thank-you note. Certain other tricks in selling the package, *you,* are not so well known. How well do you think you can sail through a job interview? Perhaps you can learn a thing or two by taking the following quiz.

1. The best homework you can do to prepare for the interview is
   A. review, in detail, your own accomplishments so you won't leave anything out.
   B. check out the company in a professional journal or the Dun & Bradstreet Directory or speak with knowledgeable people to discover its particular emphasis and growth directions.

    C. get the interview out of your mind. Get drunk or something. Worrying and planning will only make you tense.

2. Many professionals advise you to role-play an interview before the actual event. The best way to do this is to
    A. have a friend play the interviewer asking you questions. Don't giggle when you answer.
    B. take a drama course to perfect your responses and timing.
    C. ask the company, a week prior to the interview, for a list of possible questions they may ask. This will show your skill at preparedness and will, indeed, actually prepare you.
    D. intensely visualize the possible interview at night, in bed. Play it through in your mind over and over, and watch yourself answering questions smoothly.

3. Still other experts advise that you prepare with what they call the "worst-case" scenario. This means
    A. telling yourself, over and over, "I'm the worst case I ever heard of." This will calm you and prepare you for the interview.
    B. telling the interviewer all the worst cases of ineptitude on jobs that you can think of, and how you'd manage better. You thus give the interviewer a practical look at your strengths.
    C. thinking of every terrible thing that can possibly be said by the interviewer, and psyching yourself up to be prepared for it, as in, "What's the worst thing that can happen? He can say he knows I've been fired from my last job. What would happen then? Well then, I'd say that I can offer recommendations by many in the company, and that the firing was because of a personality difference between me and the boss. What else could he say? Well, he could say—"

4. OK. You walk into the interviewer's office. He greets you at the door and asks you to take a seat. You case the joint and choose

A. the chair in back of the desk.
B. the chair in front of the desk.
C. the couch.
D. the edge of the desk.
E. to stand.

5. You sit down,
   A. crossing your arms and your legs.
   B. crossing your legs and leaning back in your seat.
   C. forward on the edge of the seat with anticipation and alertness.
   D. trying not to fart with nervousness.

6. The first words spoken are
   A. by you. You ask a smart question about the company.
   B. by him.
   C. by your mother. Her voice in your head tells you to sit up straight.

7. The telephone rings. He takes it and speaks for a lengthy period. You
   A. sit very still so you won't disturb him, and remain pleasant looking.
   B. drum your fingers quietly. That gives him the unspoken message that your time is also valuable.
   C. cough a lot or clear your throat to get his attention back.
   D. stand and inspect the books in the bookcase behind you.

8. He asks if you liked your last job and why you left. You say,
   A. "I disagreed violently with the president of the company."
   B. "I initiated two successful advertising campaigns, and felt it was time to move on."
   C. "I loved everyone but hated the long hours."
   D. "I never met such a thieving, conniving bunch of crooks in my life."
   E. "It was unfulfilling."

9. He asks you how much money you're making now. (You're making $25,000.) You say,
   A. "$25,000."
   B. "$50,000."
   C. "In the range of $30,000."
   D. "That's for me to know and you to find out."

10. He takes a cigarette and offers one to you. You say,
    A. "Not on your life. My aunt got cancer from smoking."
    B. "No, thanks."
    C. "Thanks, I believe I will."
    D. "Thanks, but I only smoke Camels."

11. He looks at his watch as you describe your past accomplishments. You
    A. look at *your* watch and politely cut the interview short, saying you have another appointment. This way, you retain control of the situation.
    B. say, "Pardon *me* for boring you."
    C. switch to another, more interesting accomplishment.
    D. ask *him* a question that's relevant to the company.

12. Looking the interviewer straight in the eye
    A. is a challenging and rather rude thing to do.
    B. implies forthrightness.
    C. is impossible to keep up.
    D. produces an eye tic.

13. The interviewer asks about your ultimate career objective. You say,
    A. "*Your* job looks interesting."
    B. "Guess."
    C. "I want to start my own business, but that's far in the future."
    D. "I want to remain in this business at the highest level I can reach."
    E. "Porno rock."

14. Should you be completely aboveboard and honest in an interview?
    A. yes
    B. no

15. On leaving, what kind of handshake should you give?
    A. A woman should give a delicate handshake. (A powerful handshake would be masculine.)
    B. firm
    C. a two-handed shake, the newest thing to imply sincerity: Grasp the interviewer's outstretched hand in your hands and squeeze warmly.
    D. as hard as you can muster without appearing to strain, giving the impression of strength

ANSWERS AND ANALYSIS

1. *B* is best. Now you can sound intelligent and a potential asset to the company.

2. *A* or *D* are the right answers. *D* is a tactic that many athletes use before a competition; to visualize oneself winning is often a self-fulfilling prophecy. If you answered *C,* don't bother showing up for the interview.

3. *C* is correct. This prepares you for every possibility, and shows that you won't die from the "worst case"—very reassuring to know.

4. *B* is right. The standard place to sit is facing the interviewer. It is proper for him to control the interview. If you chose *A,* dummy, you're sitting in *his* seat—not an auspicious beginning. The couch would force him to sit next to you, implying an equality that is not yet appropriate. The edge of his desk (*D*) is far too informal. Standing (*E*) makes everyone ill at ease.

5. *B* is the most relaxed position. *A* looks hostile and overaggressive. *C* looks overanxious and nervous. *D* is the least you can do.

6. *B* is correct. It's his game.

7. *D* is the most natural, and also gives him the most privacy.

8. *B* gives you a pat on the back as well as a good reason to leave—at *your* instigation. *A* pinpoints you as a disruptive force, *C* as a lazy force, *D* as a victim, and *E* as somewhat unrealistic.

9. *No one* who knows anything *ever* tells exactly how much she's making at the old job. The interviewer doesn't even expect you to be utterly candid; he'll automatically take off five thousand from whatever you tell him. The answer, then, is *C*, which is a range and not an actual lie—a perfectly acceptable answer.

10. *B*, whether or not you smoke. That's a silent rule of the interview game.

11. *D*. Nothing awakens interest faster than being asked a question to which you know the answer.

12. *B* and *C* are both correct. Some people are so brainwashed with the cliché of looking someone in the eye, they'll never let eye contact go. That's wild. It's really OK to look away, up, at a picture, *every now and then* during the conversation. But for the most part look the interviewer in the eye.

13. *D* is correct.

14. No. Paint the prettiest picture you can without actually lying. This is not the time for either brutal candor or modesty.

15. *B* is best. *C* is silly and unprofessional. *D* will hurt the interviewer. If you answered *A* seriously, you live in the dark ages.

SCORING

Give yourself 10 points for every savvy answer.

If you scored 130–150 points, you'll sail through the interview. You know how to present yourself to best advantage with just the right amount of "cool." Even if you're not rich, powerful, or important, the interviewer sees you as a force to be reckoned with. You have the "look of success" in your body language and in your quiet, firm, positive attitude. You really ought to get the job, so relax!

If you scored 100–120, you have great potential, but need to do some brushing up in putting your best face forward. The interviewer may well be able to "smell" your fear, because body language and lack of assertiveness give you away. Read Julius Fast's book, *Body Language* (Pocket Books, 1983) and any one of the million books available on how to pass a job interview; these contain valuable pointers on selling yourself. You need to learn how to glamorize your image rather than stick to the dry nitty-gritty of facts. Work may be very important to you, and you may work very well, but you need a little more confidence to pass that interview glowingly.

If you scored 70–90, you really have a pretty unsophisticated idea of what makes a good impression. Are you planning on wearing four-inch heels to the interview? Don't. Do you still say things like, "Wow, that's heavy," or "This job sounds O-KAAY," at an interview? Don't. And forget candor at an interview. It's inappropriate and a killer. No one needs or wants to know that you have irregular periods and are prone to moodiness. What an interviewer wants to know is how you'll fit into the organization and whether you can add something to it rather than detract from the image. Get someone you admire (or take a course) to help you polish rough edges and sell your abilities.

If you scored under 70, I certainly hope your dad has a good business and doesn't insist on an interview before hiring you.

18

What's Your Worth at Work?

What are you worth to your boss? More than what you're paid? Less? Let's face it: In the working world, you're often judged by the amount of money you bankroll. It's not enough to be loved at work; if you're worthy, you should be financially appreciated. Some of us are worth quite a lot but simply don't have the courage to demand pay that reflects that worth. Others are worth very little to an employer, perhaps because they're unimaginative, unskilled, or uninterested. Take this quiz to see what you're worth at work—and if you're fairly compensated.

1. Your boss asks you to handle an account you know nothing about. You
   A. are honest and say that you wouldn't do justice to the client.
   B. say yes and quickly run to find out everything you can about the account.
   C. say you're overloaded and suggest a knowledgeable colleague.

2. In the last two years you've received at least
   A. one substantial raise.
   B. one substantial promotion but either no raise or only a token one.

C. one substantial offer from another firm.

D. one substantial sexual proposition from the boss.

3. What comes closest to your work situation?
   A. "I regularly get raises at a modest, set rate."
   B. "I get substantial raises when I ask for a well-deserved one."
   C. "A raise? Me? I'm lucky they keep me."
   D. "The boss agrees I surely deserve a raise but has asked me to wait just a bit until the economy brightens."

4. If you were the boss for a day and had to hand in an evaluation of yourself, the word you would probably use is
   A. imaginative.
   B. hardworking.
   C. peculiar.
   D. delightful.
   E. dependable.

5. If you needed a recommendation, you would first go to your
   A. best friend.
   B. psychiatrist.
   C. employer.
   D. nana.

6. Your boss
   A. rewards you.
   B. appreciates you.
   C. lusts for you.
   D. doesn't know you exist.

7. How many times have you initiated a new project this year?
   A. once
   B. more than once
   C. never
   D. Does making a romantic conquest count?

8. You're usually the one who finds the lost papers at the office, keeps the best records, works overtime when needed. In return, you get

    A. eternal gratitude.

    B. angry stares from jealous colleagues.

    C. big bucks.

    D. perfume and other lovely gifts.

    E. *bupkis* (Yiddish word for *zilch*).

9. This week, you've given your boss a
    A. spastic colon.
    B. way out of trouble.
    C. thorough week's work.
    D. hickey.

10. How many career goals did you meet this year?
    A. all of them
    B. some of them
    C. "I forget what goals I made."

11. This best sums up my feelings about work:
    A. "I so love my work that I'm willing to give up good pay for good satisfaction."
    B. "Ho hum."
    C. "I am constantly challenged, but somewhat dissatisfied with my pay scale."
    D. "I'm overqualified for the work I do."
    E. "It stinks."

12. Somehow or other, you always seem to be absolutely correct when it comes to evaluating a new client or office project. Your boss says you have
    A. fabulous luck.
    B. woman's intuition.
    C. divine judgment.
    D. violet (or blue or brown) eyes to die from.

SCORING

1. A=0,   B=5, C=2,

2. A=5,   B=2, C=5,   D=0

3. A=3,   B=5, C=−2, D=1

 4. A=5,   B=2, C=−3, D=1,   E=3
 5. A=3,   B=0, C=5,   D=−2*
 6. A=5,   B=2, C=0,   D=−1
 7. A=4,   B=5, C=0,   D=0
 8. A=0,   B=0, C=5,   D=0,   E=0
 9. A=−1, B=5, C=4,   D=0
10. A=3,   B=5, C=0
11. A=2,   B=1, C=5,   D=2,   E=0
12. A=0,   B=0, C=5,   D=−1

* unless your nana is Rose Kennedy, in which case add 5.

If you scored 55-60 points, you are really worth your weight in gold at work. People who score very high in job worth are generally so committed to their work that they find much of their personal identity in their career. You're a self-starter, creative, and on a fast track to the top—and everyone knows it. You should be making top dollar in your profession, and if you aren't, I bet you're savvy enough to look for greener fields where your stellar work will be rewarded with the salary you so richly deserve.

If you scored 45-54, you're a fine worker but perhaps not quite as aggressive as you should be in asking for your worth in dollars as well as respect. You need to take more control of your progress, because your work output is clearly of great benefit to others. Ask and ye shall receive. Expect recognition. If you don't get it, explore other work options.

If you scored 35-44, you're either not in the right job for your talents, afraid to take risks, or extremely lazy. If it's the first, don't allow yourself to be trapped on a treadmill that is boring and not encouraging of the best you can be. Try a talk with your boss to see if you can shift your job focus, or else consider some vocational testing to find a new career. If you're afraid to take risks, a job will always be just a job to you; don't blame your lack of progress on anyone else. Find an occupation or niche where you can be valuable and feel worthy; that means everything. If your problem is laziness, get your tail moving before you're out on it! You have potential for job worth: Use it!

If you scored 1-34, you're a cog in a wheel—replaceable by another anonymous cog. How come you don't give more? Only *you* know.

If you had a minus score—forget it; you're a disaster area for any employer. Better plant nice flowers in your garden and find a rich patron.

19

Are You the Boss Type?

Look, not everyone has to be Ruler of the World. There are bosses and there are workers, and both have been known to be content with their positions in the hierarchy. However, if you want to be a boss, you better make sure you have the work habits and personality traits that come along with that job description. A boss must have a strong sense of self, strong enough to be able to wield authority over others, to expect cooperation and even obedience. What's more, a boss must be able to assume responsibility in making choices—and better make the right choices most of the time.

Take the quiz below to see if you have the temperament to be top honcho.

1. There's a big job to be done. The best way to handle it is to
   A. get A to do something, B to do something else, and C to finish it up.
   B. do it yourself. Always. Anything else is crazy. You know you can't trust anyone to do the kind of work you're capable of.
   C. hire a professional for consultation on the best way to

tackle it. It's wiser to spend a little more to get the very best.

   D. take a snooze.

2. I generally feel that my decisions
   A. should not be questioned.
   B. are always open for reasonable discussion.
   C. are a reflection of group policy.
   D. are very foolish.

3. When it comes to taking big risks,
   A. don't.
   B. it's best to be cautious.
   C. it's best to take an informed chance.
   D. it's best to get a consensus opinion first.

4. If you are management, in order to be popular you should
   A. always try to explain the reasons *why* you ask the workers to do something.
   B. be warm and friendly and supportive.
   C. always remember to give a bond when a worker's son or daughter is getting married or graduating.
   D. ignore popularity. You shouldn't *have* to be liked.

5. It's not smart to make deals or trade favors with business associates to further your own career objectives.
   A. true
   B. false

6. Which of the following people do you feel you most understand?
   A. George Steinbrenner
   B. Dagwood Bumstead
   C. John DeLorean
   D. Archie Bunker
   E. Lou Grant
   F. Mary Richards

7. What counts in management success?
   A. fear—that is, how much of it you can instill in your workers

B. clothes and personal appearance
C. learning about other parts of the industry even if you're not directly involved in them
D. intellectual ability
E. being a great bluffer

8. If you were physically qualified, which would you rather be in the world of sports?
A. a member of a hockey team
B. a wide receiver on a football team
C. a quarterback on a football team
D. a volleyball player
E. a bat girl

9. Marjorie Robbins is a young lawyer starting a new job in a hotshot firm of older lawyers. Her first day, she asks her assistant to leave a half hour later than he is in the habit of doing, changes the desk placement of her secretary, and criticizes the work of an older lawyer who is nevertheless subordinate to her. Marjorie is
A. extremely pushy.
B. assertive.
C. headed for trouble.
D. acting terribly masculine.

10. Which design appeals to you the most?

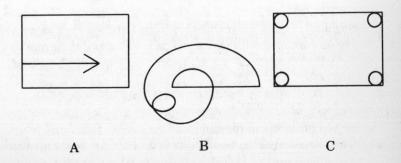

A   B   C

ANSWERS AND ANALYSIS

1. *A* is the answer: Bosses have to know how to assign responsibility. No one can do everything herself, so *B* is incorrect. *C* is foolish. You're supposed to be the authority, unless the problem is so far outside the usual sphere of operations it would be impossible to make intelligent decisions yourself—and that's unusual.

2. *A* is correct. A boss should try to communicate well with workers, but should not need group input for final decisions, as undemocratic as that sounds. A high percentage of right decisions should convince you to trust your own judgment.

3. People in management positions must be prepared to risk, says every expert in the field, so *C* is correct. It's a good idea to research the chances of success and take *intelligent risks*—but nothing ventured, very little gained.

4. *D* is correct. It's nice to be expert at human relations, and that surely helps the atmosphere of the workplace, but a person who needs to be popular and well loved can never make the unpopular decisions a boss often must make.

5. The statement is *false* (*B*). Furthering one's own career objectives is, according to experts, a very real need of most management people. Those who are content to stay in the same place don't have the aggressiveness they need to be leaders.

6. *A, C,* and *E* are all people who have the aggressiveness, authority, and charisma needed to be a boss—whether or not you like or admire them. If you can *understand* their motives, though, you probably are motivated by a need to be a leader yourself.

7. *B, C,* and *E* are all correct. Your style in clothing is symbolic of your position, whether or not you like the idea. An executive at IBM simply doesn't wear jeans or sexually provocative clothing to the office. As for *C,* a boss also is interested in a long-range and wide-scope look at the work, not

just a myopic look at the area in which she or he is involved. If you want to move up in the ranks, you surely ought to know the whole picture. Being a bluffer (*E*) is also a useful tool. Bluffing is not lying; it's using one's imagination to create impressions, a kind of creative ability to convince. That's good for bosses.

8. *C* is the only player who calls the shots.

9. *C* is the reasonable answer. If Marjorie were male, certainly her actions would be looked on as reasonable for a bright, aggressive young man. Marjorie has clearly profited from feminist teachings.

10. *B* was the answer that a test group of senior management people almost invariably chose, because it seemed more creative, more interesting. People who worked happily in a nonmanagerial position seemed to go for *A* (a clear, even, parallel path with no direction up or down) or *C* ("The circles in the corners seem protected," said several people). The design of *B* is the least contained by boundaries, the most free, the most experimental.

SCORING

Each answer is worth 10 points.

If you scored 90–100 points, you are clearly a person with executive skills. You think in terms of long-term career growth, not just holding on to a job. You're comfortable with "boss" status, and would rather work out solutions and ways to implement them than be told what to do. Your personal style says, "Take charge," and you can manage a team with innovative force. You plan, organize, and direct with grace.

If you scored 60–80, you have leadership ability, but tend to become a bit nervous when asked to take on great responsibility. You are too nice to hurt others' feelings or give firm direction. This is a skill you need to work on because a boss sometimes has to hurt feelings and always has to give direction. You have to learn how to generate work rather than complete a project someone else has started. A management-training course might be helpful, and some reading in the plethora of books on the subject is advisable.

If you scored under 60, you're happier and feel safer with a career "superior" calling the shots. You can still be a terrific, original person—you just don't love being boss. When you come home from work, you want it to be over. (Work's never really over for bosses, it's never far from their minds.)

20

Should You Have an Office Romance?

It used to be that the office romance was looked down on as a poor moral and corporate move. Inevitably, the woman involved in such a liaison would be the loser. Today, very often, Cupid is definitely on the payroll, and company time is advantageously spent on libido as well as profits. But you've got to have a knack for it if it is to work. Unless you understand the rules of the office romance, the love that flourishes in the rough-and-tumble business climate can end up giving you a kick in the corporate pants, not to mention depression both economically and emotionally.

Are you cut out for having romance on the job? Take this quiz and see.

The idea in this quiz is to give not the *nicest* answers but the ones that show you have the personality to carry off an office romance with no loss to psychological well-being or job performance.

1. The best person with whom to have an office romance is
   A. the stockboy.
   B. a peer (someone who's up and coming, just as you are).
   C. the boss (someone who's already up and would like to be coming).

   D. your mentor (someone who guides you and paves the way).

2. If you *are* having an affair with the boss, you should expect
   A. new ground rules at the office.
   B. the same old ground rules.
   C. a longer lunch hour.

3. Office romances work best when the participants are
   A. not married to other people.
   B. not competitive with each other.
   C. very competitive with each other.

4. What is your relationship with your fellow office workers?
   A. You're a member of the "in" group.
   B. You're friendly but rather aloof.
   C. You're beloved by all.
   D. You're roundly hated.

5. Your reputation for being closemouthed is
   A. laughable.
   B. well founded.
   C. nonexistent.

6. It's most likely that an office romance can mean
   A. enormous strain.
   B. interesting perks.
   C. a terrible reputation.

7. An office affair ought to be
   A. conducted with responsibility for your lover.
   B. conducted with responsibility for yourself.
   C. an experiment for probing marriage.
   D. catered.

8. When you know people are whispering about you, you
   A. feel paranoid and insecure.
   B. are basically uninterested.
   C. are secretly titillated and pleased.
   D. become angry.
   E. take more showers.

9. Hitching your sexual wagon to an office superstar is
   A. celestial.
   B. risky.
   C. advantageous.

10. You've worked hard to get places in your career. Now, the boss has to make a choice in order to fill a great, new job: It's between you and your lover. You
    A. vomit.
    B. scratch and kick to get the job.
    C. do everything to see your lover gets the job, even though you would be sorely disappointed.
    D. remove yourself from the competition by opting for another attractive position.

11. What's your opinion? The office is a fertile field for romance because
    A. it's taboo. The "don't mix work with play" ethic is strong.
    B. it's seductive. People who speak the same language and are involved in the same quests often appeal to each other.
    C. the office can be boring. Affairs inject mundane work with adrenaline.
    D. it improves teamwork.

12. You're a highly successful business achiever. You've had a number of satisfying sexual liaisons at work. Only trouble is, you keep losing your man—to his wife, to his work, to his homosexual lover, to his mother. The reason?
    A. You are too threatening and even a little "masculine" because of your power at work.
    B. You really don't want him.
    C. Your breath.

13. Office romances, these days, often lead to
    A. aggravation.
    B. mergers.
    C. crabs.

ANSWERS AND ANALYSIS

The B's have it; every B is the correct answer. Here's why.

1. The boss has too much power over you: When you break up you can fall farther than out of his bed. Your mentor should have a father-like responsibility for your success. Too much intimacy is dangerous to the relationship. The stockboy's just too young for you, Marlene.

2. Don't expect favoritism or a difference in attitude once you're outside the bedroom. It would be enormously unprofessional and destructive to office morale.

3. It's hard to be romantic two hours after you've been out for his throat. *A* is a distinct possibility, also. Give yourself half credit if you chose it.

4. Carrying off an office romance implies strong individuality. An in-crowd groupie heavily involved in office socialization and politics can't remove herself enough for the privacy such a romance requires. And if you're disliked, the gossip over such a romance will be vicious.

5. Being closemouthed is a necessity for an office romance.

6. If you *can* carry it off with style, you will have new exhilaration at the office, someone to stick up for you, and possibly tête-à-têtes and phone calls on the company tab as you work for the common good.

7. You shouldn't expect fidelity or passionate loyalty in an office fling, nor should you be expected to give it. That's the nature of the thing when it's not at a serious stage. Responsibility for yourself is all the mature person ought to consider. An affair is not a commitment or a marriage and both parties ought to understand that.

8. The office grapevine ought to be of little concern to you. If you don't have the class and psychic strength to ignore it, don't tempt it.

9. You may end up hitched to a falling star, not a rising one. It's always risky to cavort in a superstar's constellation unless you're willing to ride with the ups and downs.

10. If you're not loyal to your own career needs, you should not be out there working. Some people are better off separating work from play.

11. They're *all* correct, even *D*. A recent university study proves that people become more productive, with less tension and greater coordination and teamwork, when they are romantically involved with each other.

12. Power does not make you masculine, despite the antifeminist move to make you believe it does. Power just gives you strength—and that's seductively attractive. If you keep losing your men, clearly you're arranging it subconsciously because you have no desire for permanent alliances.

13. Yes, surprisingly enough, the office affair often does lead to marriage—as well as other mergers. Read the social announcements in your local newspaper and see how many couples met at work. The office affair often goes public!

SCORING

Give yourself 10 points for every correct answer.

If you tallied up 110–130 points, don't waste another minute. Go meet him behind the water cooler. You'll thrive on an office romance!

If you scored 80–100 points, love at the Christmas party is a distinct possibility for you, but psych yourself up to understand the stakes involved in what can be a very impermanent coupling. Can you still be friends after a fling? It's essential.

If you scored only 60–70, forget the whole thing unless you can really reconstitute your personality. People like you are too intense and too needy of permanence and promises to succeed with an affair at work.

If you scored under 60, don't even talk to attractive men at work. You'll fall on your face like a ton of bricks after the affair, because you will have misunderstood the whole thing. You need Romeo, not Burt Reynolds.

21

Do You Have
Job Burnout?

You wake up one morning, and suddenly going to work seems pointless. You're apathetic, bored, unmotivated. What's more, your job performance has been noticeably deteriorating and your stress level noticeably accelerating. Have you had it? Are you a victim of job burnout? Take this quiz to see how serious your symptoms are.

1. You remember feeling really excited about the clients of the firm and the other people with whom you work. Now, it seems
   A. you are looking at everyone from a great distance.
   B. you're angry much of the time because it's clear they no longer appreciate your work.
   C. you're sad, and deeply envious of one specific person who seems to be taking over your territory.

2. Which of these statements has rung true for you at work, at least twice this week?
   A. "I've stolen something to get even."
   B. "I've watched the clock, yawned, daydreamed, and taken a long coffee break."
   C. "I've noticed someone else doing inferior work."

3. Your mother needs to be driven to the doctor again and your daughter wants to play with someone—you. Meanwhile, it's you who have had a minor crisis at work this week. You
   A. shove your mother. Grip your daughter's arm—*hard*.
   B. swallow hard and do what seems to make them feel happier.
   C. pack up your troubles in your old kit bag and manage to have a great time with both of them.

4. What do you really want in bed?
   A. a good night's sleep
   B. an inspiration on how to start your own business
   C. an inspiration on how to beat your arch-rival out
   D. an inspiration on how to escape to Tahiti

5. What's the response you would make to this statement? "Every job has many duties that are boring and seemingly pointless."
   A. "Correct. That's common sense."
   B. "Being inflexible about what you'll do or won't do may well cost you the job—boring as it is."
   C. "I don't give a damn who knows that I hate making coffee for the bastard, and I hate this stupid job."
   D. "Wrong."

6. This is the story of your life:
   A. "I've been smoking pot (or drinking or bingeing on food) a lot lately."
   B. "All I seem to want to do is make love."
   C. "My work is so demanding, aggravating, and time consuming that every moment away from it is time wasted."
   D. "Boring. Everything's boring. Even this quiz is boring."
   E. "I am constantly exhausted. I can't sleep enough."

7. You feel
   A. certain that you have job burnout even though your job performance level has never been higher.

138

B. stress. Stomach gripers. Pains around your heart.
C. blocked and listless, as you've felt for weeks. Still, to-morrow is another day, and common sense says your job interest will pick up.
D. that some days are definitely more productive than others.
E. sterile. Without ideas.

8. You believe that
   A. work is how you keep the Devil away.
   B. work is for the lower classes.
   C. an interested and effective worker maintains a consistently good job performance, day after day.
   D. chocolate gives you pimples.

9. Choose the first words that come to mind when you read the following two words: MONDAY MORNING.
   A. trapped
   B. Hooray!
   C. Take birth-control pills.
   D. doomed
   E. TUESDAY MORNING

10. "I'd quit my job if
    A. I weren't so lazy."
    B. I weren't afraid I wouldn't find another job."
    C. I weren't the boss."
    D. it didn't make me rich."
    E. it didn't keep me interested."

ANSWERS AND ANALYSIS

The following "right" answers are not right at all—for your well-being. They indicate a high level of job boredom, stress, frustration—in short, job burnout.

1. The answer is *A*. Emotional withdrawal and lack of human connection to people you work with is a classic burnout symptom.

2. *B* is the answer that indicates boredom. *A* indicates childlike but not bored behavior, and *C* an *active* if critical interest in work—not a burnout symptom.

3. *A* is the answer. Irritation and lack of patience with those you love is another burnout signal. If you picked *C*, you may not have burnout but you're nauseatingly nice. Shove your old kit bag.

4. Either *B* or *D* is a burnout signal. Running away or fantasizing that your own business will be pressure-free are signs of job despair. *Acting* on creating your own business, in daylight hours, is healthy, and means you're taking positive steps. Fantasizing at night is a powerless thing to do.

5. The answer is *A, B,* or *C. A* shows you're resigned to witless boredom. *B* shows you're fearful of losing your security, no matter how despairingly dull your days are. *C* shows impatience with preserving outward appearances, a poor tactic that's quite common with people who have burnout: They lose all "job smarts." Only *D* indicates a person who won't put up with a vacuum at work.

6. *A, B,* and *E* are all responses from burnout victims: They seem to have fallen back on old, familiar security blankets to alleviate depression at work. Only *C* indicates a person who, although perhaps a workaholic, is definitely not burned out.

7. Every response *but A* and *D* represents burnout possibility. *A* is not burned out—no matter what she thinks—because burnouts cannot do well when they're emotionally drained and dulled. *D* also is not a burnout response—just reality. If you chose *C*, you're hopeful but wrong. You can't be really burned out and then miraculously recover without having done something about it. That's pie-in-the-sky thinking.

8. *C* is the answer that represents burnout. If you saddle yourself with impossible expectations, you're headed for performance overload and huge disappointment leading to job burnout.

9. If you chose *A* or *D*, obviously work is not your favorite place to be. If you chose *E*, it signifies nothing more than a rather limited imagination.

10. *A, B, C,* or *D* (surprise!) *could* all indicate a high degree of job burnout. The only reason to be involved and excited at work is if it's interesting. Nothing else listed is a good reason to remain at a job you dislike.

SCORING

Give yourself 10 points for every "right" answer you chose.

If you scored 90-100 points, you're a classic case of job burnout. Don't settle for being a lobotomized victim. Think about changing careers, or environments or responsibilities within the same career, before your performance, stress, and happiness levels really dive. You're in a true dead end. It's downright depressing. *Do something!* Burnout rarely gets better by itself.

If you scored 70-80, you might rethink your career and decide what to do. Perhaps all you need to enliven it are some new contacts or possibly even a good talking-out with family, boss, or friend to help you focus on what's missing. Don't suffer in silence. Your job life needs spicing up. You must take control. Leave if you have to: Temporary joblessness may spur you to a more creative future.

If you scored 40-60, you're not a ball of fire at work, but then again you're not exactly stagnant either. Maybe you just need a vacation. Or a new project. Or a new lover. Vary *something,* take a risk, make a change, before vague job dissatisfaction turns into torpor.

If you scored under 40, stop complaining. Every day doesn't have to bring you a testimonial dinner about your choice of career and your worth and contentment at work. Sounds like you've got a good deal going in terms of career.

22

Are You a Good Credit Risk?

Your banker may love and admire you for your sterling qualities and your cute sense of humor, but just try to get the loan to buy that house without a good credit rating. What's more, American Express, your favorite department store, or even your library won't be thrilled to have you on their rosters without proper credit. Your fiscal future demands that you create, add to, and protect your financial credit rating. Unfortunately, too many of us otherwise hotshot survivors don't know beans about establishing and keeping credit.

Do you know how to make your financial name as good as gold? If you don't have a good credit reputation, why not?

1. The best way to get a good credit rating is to
   A. borrow money.
   B. give excellent references.
   C. dress fashionably and have a cheery smile.
   D. sign a pledge of morality.

2. If you're thinking of taking out a large bank loan, the loan officer will
   A. probably be on the take. Offer her or him a substantial gift.

141

B. look askance at all your department-store charge accounts, which show a spendthrift personality.

C. look with favor on all your department-store charge accounts, which show you purchase on credit and repay your debts.

D. have no right to ask you why you want to borrow the money.

E. not need to make a credit check on you if you're the president or vice-president of a company.

3. You're new to all this and have not yet established that you're a good credit risk. Your bank won't loan you money for your new car. The best thing to do is

A. hold up the bank.

B. put the bite on a rich relative.

C. go to a private loan company even though you may have to pay a bit more.

D. use up your savings to buy the car. Next year, after more time on the job, you'll be able to get the loan.

4. If a lending institution says it can't advance you money because it has gotten a poor credit rating on you from your local credit bureau, you have an absolute right to

A. ask the credit bureau to give you a written report on your file.

B. sue the lending institution.

C. sue the credit bureau.

D. bomb the credit bureau.

5. A cosigner is someone

A. who designs fashion clothing.

B. who will pay off your loan—like a parent.

C. who will back your loan financially.

D. responsible, from your company, who will sign a reference.

6. If you are a housewife,

A. your spouse's excellent credit references automatically revert to you when you want credit cards in your own name.

B. this laziness might be held against you when you try to obtain credit.

C. it's a good idea to build up your own credit history, if possible, by getting bank accounts and charge cards in *your* name (not your spouse's).

D. you cannot have credit cards in your own name. No one can without a paying job.

7. A banker in a lending institution from which you are requesting a loan has every right to ask you

A. your race and religion.

B. whether you're widowed or divorced.

C. how much money you already owe.

D. your plans for a family or your birth-control methods (to determine if you're likely to become pregnant and leave your job, thereby jeopardizing the loan repayment).

E. out on a date.

8. Your credit rating is greatly enhanced if you're able to

A. pay for everything in cash.

B. pay bills immediately after getting a dunning notice.

C. use your credit cards to buy things—even things you could easily pay for in cash—and pay the bill as soon as you receive it.

D. marry J. Paul Getty.

9. If you've had problems in the past with your credit and want to start over with a clean slate with a new lending institution, it's a good idea

A. —without actually lying—not to *offer* any information about your past credit problems.

B. to open a new bank account and get new charge accounts, and use them responsibly for a few months before applying.

C. to get an alias.

10. If you determine, after inspection, that a credit bureau has wrong or misleading information on you,

A. you're stuck. Tough luck. Perhaps you can convince a

potential creditor that the information he has been given is wrong.

B. there are a number of steps that you can take to erase inaccuracies on your credit rating.

C. ask to have your records handled by another credit bureau.

ANSWERS AND ANALYSIS

1. *A* is definitely correct. Even if you don't need the money, it's a good idea to borrow $300 or $400 from a bank or credit union, let it sit in a savings account and reap interest, and then pay it back promptly on the due date. Borrowing through charge plates at the local department store, and of course paying back on time, is another way to establish a credit rating.

2. *C* is the only correct answer. If you try *A,* forget getting a decent credit rating.

3. *C* is the right answer. To establish credit, first you have to get someone else to lend you money—and no one likes to be first. Try a lending company like CIT, Beneficial Finance, or Household Finance. They may charge you a bit more, but it's worth it. Just make sure you pay it back on time—or even before—for it to count in your favor! Using up your savings (*D*) is silly because it will do nothing to establish credit, and you'll end up in the same bind as before (minus the savings).

4. *A* is correct. Credit bureaus are required to disclose any derogatory information that appears on your record, if you ask for it. (See the 1971 Fair Credit Reporting Act.) You *can* sue, of course, but unless you can prove damages you won't win.

5. *C* is the right answer. The cosigner is just as liable as the signer to make sure the debt gets paid. However, having a cosigner pay off your debt is not terrific for your credit rating.

6. *C* is the only answer. Don't depend on your spouse. I know widows who charged purchases for forty years and paid off faithfully using their husband's cards or name, and then,

upon the death of their husband, found that this was *worthless* as far as their own credit was concerned. If you chose *B*, you need your consciousness raised. Working within the home doesn't mean laziness by a long stretch. Ever see a harried mom?

7. *C* and *only C* is correct.

8. *C* is the right response. (Although *D* wouldn't do too badly for a credit rating.)

9. *B* is the answer. Never try to conceal past problems, because any lending agency that's reputable has direct access to central credit files on you. If it's proved you tell less than the truth, you'll be considered a crummy credit risk.

10. *B* is correct. Your lending institution or lawyer can tell you how to go about having erroneous information removed from your record (if you can prove it's erroneous).

SCORING

Give yourself 10 points for every correct answer.

If you scored from 80–100 points, you're a wonderful credit risk (if you weren't lying about your answers). You're informed about your rights, and probably make a great effort to keep your rating as high as possible. Even if you don't make a great deal of money, you understand exactly how to make yourself an appealing risk for any lending institution. You're a sophisticated and responsible consumer, and your credit rating is as valuable as your good name: It, financially speaking, *is* your good name.

If you scored 60–70 points, you are either not as knowledgeable as you should be about your financial rights, or you've been careless about paying your bills. Have you been overspending and charging and not paying back on time? Every time you're late with a payment it's reported on your credit account to a credit bureau—and that adds up! Keep your credit as clean as you can. It will pay off with a reputation that will get you loans and even certain positions that are dependent upon your record.

If you scored under 60, you've got problems. Either marry rich or *learn now* about balancing checkbooks and loans and credit! Right now your own mother might hesitate to loan you five bucks. Be professional and reliable!

23

Will You Ever Be Really Rich?

Years ago there was a popular weekly television program called *The Millionaire;* in each episode this very rich guy got his kicks by giving away a million dollars to a different stranger. It was popular because it fulfilled a common fantasy: Who among us has not dreamed of finding or inheriting a fortune? But inheriting or finding money is quite different from making it. Being a huge money earner or even the influence behind a huge money earner requires specific personality traits. People who have uncanny second sight as to parlaying dollars into fortunes have many characteristics in common. Are you such a person? Below is a million-dollar quiz to help you find out.

1. How much luck do you have?
   A. "None. I'm cursed."
   B. "I don't believe in luck."
   C. "As much as the next person, I guess."
   D. "An extraordinary amount."
   E. "Depends on my stars."

2. When you die, if your family is honest, your tombstone might say,
   A. "She valued truth and wisdom above all else."
   B. "Never tired, at last she rests."

C. "She was a free spirit."

D. "She was a risk taker."

E. "She lived for family and friends."

3. Your favorite of the following games is
   A. roulette.
   B. chess.
   C. doing a puzzle.
   D. poker.
   E. darts.

4. Your body needs
   A. malteds.
   B. challenges.
   C. loving.
   D. less than six hours of nightly sleep.
   E. plastic surgery.

5. In certain ways (not all, of course) you can strongly identify with
   A. Mother Teresa.
   B. Jane Fonda.
   C. your favorite teacher.
   D. Hitler.
   E. your wonderful mother who gave her all for her home.

6. At a cocktail party, you'd most likely
   A. drink copiously and embarrass someone.
   B. be the center of attention.
   C. become involved in conversation with the most handsome man there.
   D. circulate and introduce yourself to people.
   E. pass around your business card to many influential people.

7. The following statement best represents the state of my health:
   A. "I rarely get sick, but I'm smart enough to take whatever sick leave that's due me."
   B. "There is very little physical illness or stress-induced illness in my family background."

   C. "I am sick enough that I have to stay in bed four or five times a year."

   D. "I can't remember the last time I missed a day of work due to illness."

   E. "Call the specialist!"

8. If you had a million dollars, you'd
   A. retire.
   B. let everyone know.
   C. spend it.
   D. invest it.
   E. leave town.

9. You're highly skilled at
   A. being a team player.
   B. making yourself noticeable.
   C. art, music, or literature.
   D. negotiating.
   E. foreplay.

10. This is what you think of yourself:
   A. "I'm a real nerd."
   B. "I'm fabulous."
   C. "I'm nice but unfortunate looking."
   D. "I'm flexible."
   E. "I'm shy but loyal and devoted."

11. This is what you think about honesty:
   A. "Honesty is the best policy."
   B. "It's nice but not crucial that others think one is honest."
   C. "I would do something dishonest if I were sure no one would know about it."
   D. "Honesty is the best policy if it suits *my* policies."
   E. "Honesty is a waste of time."

12. If you were granted a wish right now, you would wish that your husband or lover would
   A. take a vacation.
   B. develop a problem-solving mentality.
   C. save his money.

D. work for himself.

E. have a massive erection.

ANSWERS AND ANALYSIS

D is the jackpot choice throughout (see "Scoring" below).

1. Millionaires who enjoy good "luck"—whether or not they believe in luck—are the driving forces behind that luck. People usually *make* their own luck.

2. The most common characteristic shared among self-made millionaires is that they're willing to take risks. Most of them also have boundless energy.

3. Poker relies on individual skill and the consummate talent to mislead and convince others. Chess (*B*) comes next because skill in chess relies on problem solving and thinking ahead, two talents characteristic of millionaires. Roulette and darts depend on chance and physical skill respectively—unimportant here.

4. Most millionaires don't waste a whole lot of time snoozing.

5. Hitler with his monomania and bluffing skill could have been a billionaire had he chosen money instead of evil and monstrous power. *A* is the worst choice, because saints, though good, are not moneymakers. Fonda's a good choice because she is creative and aggressive.

6. Millionaires have a talent for scouting out influential people; anyone who walks around handing business cards to many people looks like a fool.

7. Most millionaires are such workaholics that only potentially fatal illnesses can draw them away from the source of money. Having a healthy family history portends well.

8. Millionaires keep on earning. Part of their golden touch is their reputation (*B*). Others tend to take chances on someone who's made it.

9. Most millionaires can strike a terrific bargain for themselves. They also have a knack of drawing attention to themselves and their success (*B*).

10. Moneymakers can bend, experiment, be flexible with new options. They also have very high feelings of self-worth (*B*).

11. Integrity is lovely, but most top-notch moneymakers bend integrity to their own needs. They also know that others tend to overlook minor dishonesty if one is very successful and can send a little of that success their way (*B*).

12. Most millionaires are those who take the risk of going into their own business in order to reap it all rather than settle for mediocre or even good rewards in someone else's million-dollar business.

SCORING

Give yourself $0.00 for an *A* choice; $50,000 for a *B* choice; $5,000 for a *C* choice; $100,000 for each *D* choice; $1,000 for each *E* choice. Then count your fortune.

If you earned $1,000,000 or more, you're some hotshot tycoon. Even if you're not yet rich, you have the personality and drive to either get there or give someone a giant push to help *him* arrive in dollar-lotusland. Many people seek wise words or small loans from you.

If you earned from $700,000 to $975,000, you have a money-making mentality but every now and then let some little thing like scruples or family concerns get in your way. When you toughen up, you'll grow into a model mogul.

If you earned from $400,000 to $675,000, you're not in the really rich class, nor will you likely ever be. Take a nice job. Enjoy your two weeks in the mountains. Play the lottery.

If you earned under $400,000 in this quiz, you can't even afford a vacation: Better stay home and watch *Bowling for Dollars.* You're probably an English major.

24

Do You Have the Winner's Mystique?

Everyone has met her—that person who always gets the plummiest assignments, the highest raises, the most enchanting business luncheons. She's the luckiest woman in the world. You're so jealous of her luck, you're not beyond wishing bird droppings would fall on her head as she goes off to one of those luncheons.

But luck, my friends, has nothing to do with it. Career winners are made, not born, and they've carefully developed the winner's mystique that's behind all that success. Victory, like bird droppings, doesn't often fall from the sky. You make your own victories; confidence and attitude have more to do with this than luck.

Deep inside, have you the mystique of a winner or a loser? The questions below will help you to determine the answer.

1. Your finances haven't improved in two years.
   A. "It's not my fault. Others have unfairly edged me out by using influence or trickery."
   B. "I'm due for the usual 5 percent increase shortly."
   C. "So what?! Money isn't everything."
   D. "It's because I've gone out on my own in a new business."

2. You appear to be making no impression at a business meeting. That's because
   A. basically you're a bubblehead.
   B. you're wearing Gaucho pants.
   C. you're listening.
   D. you haven't done your homework.

3. True or false?
   A. Anyone can do anything she or he truly wants to do. _____
   B. Winners are careful not to take huge risks. _____
   C. Winners tend to compete with the biggest heros. _____
   D. Winners are often very annoying. _____

4. How would you find a mentor?
   A. Advertise.
   B. Ask someone if he'd like to be your mentor.
   C. Join a professional organization.
   D. "What's a mentor?"

5. You've been offered the next step up the corporate ladder, but are told that your office space, out in the open with the rest of the assistants, will remain the same. You
   A. insist that there be some change in your physical surroundings.
   B. are thrilled and flattered.
   C. understand that success and power have nothing to do with where you sit.

6. You're nervous about speaking in public. Your job demands that you do so. In order to psych yourself up, you
   A. tell yourself what a dolt you're being and how smooth a speaker you really are.
   B. join a drama or discussion group.
   C. carefully observe successful speakers and try to imitate their mannerisms.
   D. visualize yourself speaking effectively. Rehearse your speeches mentally before giving them.

7. Marilyn, your immediate superior, is moving to another firm and a wonderful new job with awesome responsibilities. She asks you to lunch. You expect her
   A. definitely to pay.
   B. to pay *and* give you a really nice gift in gratitude for your past support.
   C. to offer you a new position and a raise if you follow her to the new job.
   D. to ask you to come along as her trusted assistant.

8. People more talented than you
   A. suck.
   B. make you very nervous.
   C. inspire you.
   D. are breathing up all your air.

9. You're an executive and have been fired because a large conglomerate has just taken over your smaller company. You
   A. develop a duodenal ulcer.
   B. check the network for what's available, and let it be known that you're in the market for a change.
   C. inform family and friends you'll break the knees of anyone who reveals that you're soon to be out of a job.
   D. go immediately to an employment agency.
   E. put an ad in the paper.

10. You believe that stress
    A. is a killer.
    B. can spur you on to greater heights.
    C. comes from sausage and peppers.

11. Which of these writers had the right idea?
    A. "When I consider life, 'tis all a cheat; . . ."—John Dryden
    B. "Life is just one damned thing after another."—Frank Ward O'Malley
    C. "Life is a ladder—infinite stepped."—Joseph Warren Fabens
    D. "As for life, it is a battle . . ."—Marcus Aurelius
    E. "Life is a disease."—George Bernard Shaw

ANSWERS AND ANALYSIS

1. *D* is the answer—the *only* answer—that a winner would give. *A* signifies someone who does not assume responsibility for cause and effect. Winners know they have only themselves to thank or blame for success. A *B* answer indicates someone who is satisfied with anything thrown her way. A *C* response is one of a defensive person who thinks more of money than she's letting on.

2. *D* is the winner's response. The person who arrives at a meeting with a well-directed plan of action usually controls the meeting and gets credit for her or his ideas. People pay attention to powerhouses who happen to be momentarily listening. If they're not paying attention to you, it's probably because you're comatose in your attention. If you think you're a bubblehead, you probably are, and you *certainly* are if you wear Gaucho pants to a meeting.

3. All false. *A:* If you have a bad limp, you can't be tennis champ. Winners know themselves and their strengths, as well as their weaknesses. *B:* Winners are known to be risk takers. *C:* Winners tend to compete with themselves, with what they were yesterday, not with mythical heros. *D:* Winners are usually delightful. Winning has a way of making you an interesting person!

4. The answer is *C:* You'll be in position to meet influential and helpful people when you hang out with others in your profession. Asking someone to be your mentor is a little like asking someone to be your mommy or daddy.

5. *A* is the answer. "The extreme of nonpower is a desk in the open," says Michael Korda, author of *Power: How to Get It, How to Use It* (Random House, 1975). It's important to have an office and your own space. If you can't get that, you must get *some* change in your physical surroundings as a sign of your improved position.

6. Either *B* or *D* is correct. *B* will give you useful practice in public speaking, and *D* is a technique many winners use. "Imaging success," as Norman Vincent Peale calls it—that is,

visualizing an action done correctly—seems to make the real thing happen. Just observing other winners (*C*) won't make you one.

7. *C* is the answer. If she offers a step up, your work and loyalty have paid off. If she offers only another supporting role, you've won nothing, right? Winners instinctively go for the advancement. Settling for lunch indicates a peon.

8. *C* is the winner's response. All other answers indicate a "mystique" geared to mediocrity.

9. *B* is correct. Smart-money executives don't get crippled by executive turnover—it happens all the time. Failing to keep one job doesn't indicate a failure. They also know that no top executive finds her or his job through the Yellow Pages, Employment Agencies, or advertising—or by being secretive. The name of the game is the old-boy/old-girl network of contacts.

10. If you believe stress will surely kill you, it probably will (*A*). No, *B* is the winner's answer. No one can avoid stress all of the time, and a winner knows how to make stress work for her as an energy-giving force. A stressless person is a nerd. Actually, *too many* sausages and peppers can kill you, but they don't necessarily produce stress.

11. A winner would choose *C* or *D*. Life *is* a battle with winners and losers: Winners know and accept and expect this and prepare themselves for the excitement. Life is also a ladder with rungs pointing upward for winners. If you side with Shaw about life being a disease—well, lots of luck; you'll need it.

SCORING

Give yourself 10 points for each correct answer.

If you scored 90–110 points, you have the mystique of a winner, for sure. You've got the winning personality characteristics: confidence, aggressiveness, the instinctive ability to judge situations and people. You enjoy competition, handle stress well, and are able, if you fail, to pick yourself up and learn from the failure. Your attitude bespeaks success. People tend to buy your ideas and skills because *you* know they're worthwhile—right?

If you've scored 60-80, your mystique needs a critique. You are not tapping your strengths. Probably you are not allowing yourself to be motivated by success—perhaps because you fear the responsibilities of winning. An assertiveness course might help. Change your friends if they're losers at life, because winning people tend to inspire other winners, and losers push losing. Psych yourself up: You clearly have the potential, but your attitude needs revving up.

If you've scored 40-50, your mystique is down you-know-what creek. Why do you always make the decision that will do you in? Why do you accept so far less than what you deserve? Try setting attainable goals, one by one, and then try patting yourself on the back every time you gain a victory. Restructure your life plan: Try to win, not just survive. Concentrate on strengths—surely you have some. One or two? If you don't, develop a couple. How can you be a winner if you don't know the rules of the game?

If you've scored under 40, there's something seriously wrong with you. Forget about the winner's mystique: You're lucky if you just get on the team. Curl up, eat a Fig Newton, take a nap. You're better off not competing.